SHARPER IMAGE SUCCESS

SHARPER IMAGE SUCCESS

BUSINESS LESSONS FROM
AMERICA'S GADGET GUY

RICHARD
THALHEIMER

LIONCREST
PUBLISHING

SHARPER IMAGE SUCCESS
Business Lessons from America's Gadget Guy

ISBN   978-1-5445-1791-9 *Hardcover*
      978-1-5445-1790-2 *Paperback*
      978-1-5445-1792-6 *Ebook*
      978-1-5445-1793-3 *Audiobook*

CONTENTS

FOREWORD

It's a great gift to get a real glimpse into the complex and active mind of a successful entrepreneur. And to see the mind of a man who started his lifelong, single career business with a simple magazine ad for a single product, which later grew into a $750 million company that has been listed on NASDAQ. Fortunately, books like this one allow us to gain insight into the mindset that creates this extraordinary kind of success and longevity.

I first met Richard in 1999 at an Internet conference in Chicago. He walked up to me, steadfast and strong in his celebrity status, he was recruiting for the Head of the Internet Division for The Sharper Image, *sharperimage. com*, which was in its infancy.

We agreed to meet the next morning at The Ritz Carlton. Even though that was more than 20 years ago, I still recall the sharpness of his well-ironed suit, his gentle, warm, and pleasant attitude, and his pride and joy when he spoke about how *sharperimage.com* was pioneering the digital future.

Two months later, I took the job and moved to San Francisco. Everything about Richard and the company was magical. The precision of the way meetings were run, the classy design style of the office, and the collection of extraordinary personnel whose way of being seemed like they should all receive overachiever awards from Dale Carnegie.

I was 27 at the time, flying to Internet conferences all over the United States to speak and share facts and figures on how *sharperimage.com* was navigating click-throughs, 3D digital rendering, and the wild west of e-commerce. In that first year alone, we went from $8 million to $31 million, and I hired 22 people. The unique part of this is that Richard was willing for me to publicly share our numbers, strategies, successes, and failures. He wanted to win in his business, but he wanted the whole world of e-commerce to win, too.

Fast forward, 20 years later, we were reconnected at The Sharper Image employee reunion at his second home in Napa. I was so excited to see Richard and express my love and gratitude for how he influenced my life and my career. I knew he took a risk when he hired me. I was 27 years old at the time and although I did have a lot of Internet marketing experience, I was not a seasoned business executive. My time there was a period of great professional transformation. I was also so grateful for The Sharper Image brand—it had opened so many doors for me throughout my career.

When we had a moment to reconnect at the reunion, I remember saying to him, with a jubilant tone, "I just love you so much, thank you!" I had so much respect and honor for him and for the extraordinary entrepreneurial path he traveled.

In September 2018, I started working with Richard again. Since then, we've produced all sorts of great things together—the YouTube channel, websites, an investing community, and of course, this book.

Richard has an uncanny way of empowering people by allowing them to feel responsible for the ideas they propose. Over and over again, there are stories of employees, myself included, who had big dreams for their projects. Richard would allow the ideas to unfold—without giving a "tell" that he could see where they were going—and let the person he hired do their job.

I want you to know that Richard is the real deal. He is generous of spirit with everyone. When I think of him, I think of his extraordinary intelligence, his positive outlook on life, his engagement in making life fun, his refined taste and awareness of the finer things in life and his mindset. That's what makes him so extraordinary.

He is the expert salesperson, maverick marketer, the polished gentleman, and the wise wizard with extrasensory perception. His success and wealth didn't happen because he grabbed at it, forced it, or manipulated his way to the top.

He is gracious with everyone and commands the helm by being pleasurable and interested in people. He is always focused on being interested, not interesting. And he is still directing and encouraging others to take the lead while he empowers them.

All of these qualities are aspects of the Billionaire Mindset. There are hundreds of examples from employees, vendors, and customers who have experienced something magical in his presence. Whether it's dividing big projects into small stages, viewing failure as a teaching catalyst, or believing wealth comes to you if you help other people, he has an unparalleled positive attitude and joyous drive for fun and success.

After editing this book, I took the liberty of adding a new chapter called *Stories of Innovation*. It's a handful of stories from Sharper Image employees who are speaking about their experience with Richard. I wanted you to get a sense of who Richard is from multiple people so you could understand the context for his own stories and the value he has created by investing in great people who continue to become even greater through his style of leadership.

Employees repeatedly share that he empowered them with a big job or big project early in their career, and they grew into it and experienced a whole new version of greatness within themselves. I am grateful to be walking on that road with him right now. I love the way Richard shows up in the world, how he thinks about people, how he interacts, and how he gives people the benefit of the doubt.

He has impacted my life in so many ways. Whether it's the gentle but long pause to give others the space to share and explain first, or treating our vendors like customers or having a quick interaction with friends at the dog park while we're reviewing edits for this book, his spirit is the same. He is gentle and fun, yet firm and direct. The way he approaches life is always consistent—and it is his billionaire mindset that has stayed the same.

Whether you're starting a new business, are a seasoned entrepreneur, or you are working your way up the corporate ladder...this book is worth your time and attention because Richard's stories contain the subtleties of this Billionaire Mindset that will benefit you in every part of your life.

Ultimately, Richard teaches us that our originality, and our relationships are the most important attributes of success. He shares his techniques for connecting with others—even in conflict—but especially in negotiation and collaboration.

This book will make a difference because it's not about how to work at your computer or make your apps more efficient; it's about getting a true glimpse into the complex and active mind of a successful entrepreneur who shares stories about creating his visions, taking risks, sharing reward, cultivating generosity, and showing respect, as well as knowing there always is a way to solve every problem.

I am grateful to have edited this book for you and to introduce you to true wisdom from Richard Thalheimer, "America's Gadget Guy."

With professional admiration for my business hero,

Meredith

—Meredith Medland Sasseen

ABOUT RICHARD THALHEIMER

Richard Thalheimer led The Sharper Image to its peak as CEO with annual revenues of $750 million, 200 stores, catalogs, an online store, and 4,000 employees. The company became a public corporation in 1987 when its stock was listed on NASDAQ.

Successful Investor, The Sharper Fund: Thalheimer now runs The Sharper Fund, a successful private fund. He is a stock guru and investing expert, sought after by journalists and their readers for his trendsetting observations about products, companies, and market movements. His experience talking to analysts for 20 years as the CEO of The Sharper Image has given him great insight into how Wall Street analysts think, and consequently, when and why investors should confidently follow their judgments.

Richard is known for his preternatural ability to identify what people want, often before realizing it themselves. This intuitive ability to drive market trends coupled with an ability to spot products that could produce millions, combined with his lawyer's precision, a healthy dose of entrepreneurial drive and an eternally playful outlook, converged to give Richard Thalheimer the well-deserved title *America's Gadget Guy* in the 1980s.

A TIMELINE—TO, THROUGH, AND BEYOND THE SHARPER IMAGE

Early Life: Richard Thalheimer was raised in Little Rock, Arkansas. After graduating from Hall High School in Little Rock, Arkansas, he left for New Haven and graduated from Yale University in 1970. He entered San Francisco's Hastings Law School shortly after that.

While still a 24-year-old law student, Richard started an office supply business called Thalheimer Business Systems, with $500 worth of copier paper. He later named his enterprise **The Sharper Image** to help promote the quality of prints available from his copy machines. After graduating from law school in 1974, Richard passed the California bar exam and practiced law in San Francisco for a year. It was also evident to those around him that any business venture he put his mind to would be unique, life-enhancing, and on an impressive global scale. He was identified as a superstar early in his career.

Beginnings of The Sharper Image: Richard's business success story was launched by a $69 Realtime watch for runners, which he discovered at a 1977 Las Vegas trade show. Impressed to find a genuine chronograph that was waterproof and shock-resistant but still affordable, Richard was determined to acquire its exclusive US distribution.

This watch became the first major consumer hit of his new company, The Sharper Image. With a stroke of marketing genius, Richard convinced his friend, legendary ultra-marathoner, Walt Stack, to be featured wearing his watch in a full-page *Runner's World* ad. The headline copy grabbed the reader's attention, saying, "Finally, a chronograph that keeps up with amazing Walt Stack."

As the watch orders poured in, Richard was already one step ahead, using his legendary ability to spot the products that would connect with the child in every adult man and woman for his first mail-order catalog. He described his mission in life as, "Picking out fun toys for grown-ups."

First to Market: The "toys" Richard sought out and marketed via The Sharper Image included the precursors to what we would now consider life essentials, such as the first cordless telephone, the first telephone answering machine, the first handheld computer, and the first iPod. Others, like the Ionic Breeze and Razor scooter (the most popular gift of 2000), anticipated emerging consumer trends. In 1991, the company set up Sharper Image Design to develop and patent its own products.

The 1980s: People loved looking at, touching, and buying unusual gadgets in stores so much that The Sharper Image became one of the hottest retail success stories of the 1980s. Everyone wanted to sit in a Massage Chair!

By 1985, The Sharper Image was grossing $100 million in sales—completely self-funded, with no outside capital or debt. *The New Yorker* described Richard as the "very model of a major entrepreneur. Thalheimer is muscular, deliberate, and tenacious, and infallibly gifted at curating ridiculously niche gadgets, like a mini electric fan on a neck chain."

Razor Scooter: On an outing to search for new products, Richard spotted the Razor scooter at a toy fair in Hong Kong and brought it to the United States. He negotiated an exclusive 24-month deal and sold a million of them in the first year. It was later heralded as the most popular gift of the year 2000. Richard was personally responsible for bringing the modern scooter to the masses.

Richard Thalheimer, a Prime-Time TV Celebrity: Richard was instantly famous and appeared on prime-time talk shows and evening news broadcasts. So influential is his legacy you can still see parts of his story on YouTube from media such as Oprah, The Today Show, Good Morning America, ABC's 20/20, The Tonight Show with Jay Leno, Late Night with David Letterman, Lifestyles of the Rich and Famous, Fox News, San Francisco Weekly, Forbes, and the Wall Street Journal.

The Sharper Image catalog itself became a cultural icon and a darling of Hollywood's A-listers, many of whom Richard featured in the catalog before they were known. Movie fans spotted The Sharper Image in *The Firm* featuring Tom Cruise, *When Harry Met Sally* with Billy Crystal and Meg Ryan, *Snow Dogs* with Cuba Gooding Jr., and *Sex In the City*. Many consumers remember The Sharper Image credit card used in *A View to Kill* with Roger Moore as James Bond.

Author: Richard wrote his insights into the 2004 business book, *Creating Your Own Sharper Image*. The audio version features his voice. The book is an inspirational and educational read for aspiring entrepreneurs with much useful information still valid today.

Ongoing Successful Retail Stores: Richard pushed the company through a very risky expansion by opening nine stores in 1985 that cost about $5 million. The company's net worth was $2 million at the time. If the expansion failed, he knew The Sharper Image would be out of business. But he struck gold again, eventually opening 180 retail locations by 2005.

Publicly Traded: On February 2, 1987, The Sharper Image Corporation became a publicly listed company on the NASDAQ Stock Exchange. Years later, on April 22, 2002, Richard and several executive team members were invited to the Nasdaq Stock Exchange to ring the opening bell. At its peak, The Sharper Image employed more than 4,000 employees and had almost 200 retail stores from San Francisco to London to Tokyo.

Electronic Stores/Online Retailer: When the Internet was in its infancy, Richard saw its potential to shorten both purchase time for consumers and costs for retailers. He was quoted in early industry trades as envisioning linking phones and websites, which he termed "electronic stores."

Yet again, Richard's prescient ability proved to be true. When Richard ventured early into the brave new world of e-commerce, debates at lively strategic planning sessions were filled with his strong belief in selling on the web. He first pitched the idea of an e-commerce platform to his Board of Directors in 1995. He was rebuffed and told by one of the directors, "No one will ever spend money on the Internet."

In 1996, the online division brought in 10 times the amount of sales, compared to just one year earlier. Then, within a 60-day window in late 2006, the volume in dollars doubled; eventually, online sales became 30 percent of the company's revenues.

Richard Thalheimer and Steve Jobs: After the initial launch of *sharperimage.com* as an active e-commerce site, Steve, Richard, and their two companies worked together to develop state of the art digital display options and algorithms for The Sharper Image website.

At Internet World Expo in 1996, Richard Thalheimer and Steve Jobs presented NeXt dynamic web pages, unveiling the new Sharper Image catalog, a first in the industry. The revolutionary partnership between Richard and Steve jobs pioneered modern-day eCommerce. *Wired Magazine* wrote that Jobs' innovations and Thalheimer's vision changed the retail sector forever.

Departure: Richard left the company in 2006, after enjoying the successes of its peak annual revenues of more than $750 million. In 2007, he sold the remainder of his 21 percent stake in The Sharper Image to a hedge fund for $26 million, and he was then completely out of the company he founded. In 2008, under the new hedge fund leadership, the company filed for bankruptcy, and all of its stores closed later that same year.

Richard Goes Out on His Own: A year after stepping down from The Sharper Image, Richard started his own retail online store, *RichardSolo.com.* He continues the business as a side hobby today.

The Legend of Sharper Image Video Footage: In 2019, a YouTube Channel was launched (The Legend of Sharper Image) that contains commercials, press appearances, product updates, and behind-the-scenes business meetings demonstrating Richard's intuitive and inspiring leadership skills.

Richard Thalheimer's legacy to business, retail, and humanity is substantial and pervasive. In many ways, he revolutionized the way we create, think, live, and play and brought new excitement, quality, and innovation to the consumer experience. He single-handedly created the upscale gadget market sector.

The Sharper Fund: After studying with the Najarian Brothers, in 2010, Richard began a serious investment career. In 2015, he launched his private fund, The Sharper Fund, known for its aggressive formula, which includes put options, long call options, and holding stock positions in publicly listed US-based companies with instant liquidity. The fund published three years of performance results, featuring a YTD total return of +92% in 2017, +96% in 2019, and +161% YTD as of September 30, 2020.

Tesla Investment: Richard's Tesla investment is a case study of how he chooses stock picks. He initially visited a Tesla Showroom in 2003 when the stock was at $35. After taking a test ride, he started buying the stock. When he purchased his first Tesla Model S shortly after that, the stock was moving up. Later, he bought a second Tesla, then a third, and eventually a fourth. He continued to accumulate the stock as a result. He has now multiplied his investment many times over, making millions in the process. His published statement in December 2018 was when the stock was at $308, contradicting Bob Lutz's public position against Tesla. Richard called then for a further move up, and Tesla stock continued to soar to new heights. In 2020, Tesla continued its meteoric rise, hitting $2,213 by August 30.

Sharper Investing—Richard's Online Investing Wisdom: Richard has taken what he has learned through decades of investing and made it accessible to investors via the web. He offers investing wisdom, stock picks, and specific trading examples that inspire the first-time investor and the seasoned investor. His goal is to empower investors to skillfully trade options on their own by reducing risk and maximizing long-term gain. In his book, *Sharper Investing: Ditch Your Broker & Double Your Returns*, investors learn about his unique and simple portfolio management approach. More at *SharperInvesting.com*.

Real Estate: In 2014, Richard sold his longtime home in San Francisco for $10.1 million. His primary residence is a $20 million mansion in Ross, California, located just north of San Francisco in Marin County. He owns a second home in Sonoma County, CA.

Toys: Today, Richard regularly flies his Cessna 182 airplane around the Northwest States and rides his Harley-Davidson Tri-Glide in the hills of Marin County.

Personal Life: Richard lives in Marin County, CA, and enjoys family time with his wife, daughters, and two dogs.

ACKNOWLEDGMENTS

There are three key people I would like to acknowledge for their contribution to this book. Each of them has shown their commitment to excellence as well as their loyalty and support of my work through the years.

First, I'd like to thank and acknowledge **Meredith Medland Sasseen** of 3 Outcomes Management Group. Without her, this book would not have happened.

In 2018, I reconnected with Meredith at a Sharper Image employee reunion at my second home in Napa. Meredith was so complimentary and appreciative of the career experience she gained while working as the Director of the Internet Division for Sharper Image in the late 1990s and acknowledged the positive impact it had on her career. Her passion and commitment to the brand, and interest in my vision for the future, reminded me of her unique talent and drive. In September 2018, she began her new phase of work with me, this time as a consultant and publicist on a variety of my legacy projects.

In our present-day work together, I've enjoyed her creativity and the broad scope of knowledge. She has demonstrated her versatility and expertise while launching my personal website, *RichardThalheimer.com*, categorizing my extensive DVD collection from my career at Sharper Image on a new YouTube channel, *@LegendofSharperImage*, managing my press communications in the financial industry as well as spearheading the writing of this book and my upcoming 2021 book, *Sharper Investing: Ditch Your Broker & Double Your Returns*.

We've accomplished a lot together. She is intelligent, intuitive, fun and a pleasure to do business with. I am grateful for her commitment to preserving the legacy of The Sharper Image and for presenting the stories of the extraordinary experiences I've had along the way. Meredith, thank you for solidifying my legacy and your great attention to detail and excellence as we create even more in the future.

Next, thank you to the former EVP & Chief Security Officer of The Sharper Image, **Joe Williams**. He is responsible for evoking the memories of 22 years of working together. I remember when Joe was interviewed by CSO magazine on the importance of a successful CSO working closely with a CEO. We both share a love of flying. At the time of the magazine interview, I recall sitting in the airplane hangar as the photographer took pictures of us and realizing that Joe would always have my back.

He is someone I can really trust. Even after our days at The Sharper Image, we've continued to create memories together. We continue to fly, and these are special times when we are able to connect as admirers of airplanes and American landscapes while celebrating the achievements we had together in creating The Sharper Image. For our lifelong friendship, Joe, I am forever grateful. (And I'll always have your back, too.)

And to **Xavier Estrada** of Xavier Estrada Design, our incredible creative designer, who is the driving force on all my photo production, brand identity, and creative design for all my online projects and the cover of this book.

Xavier started working for The Sharper Image when he was 21 years old. It was his first job out of design school. He told me it was his dream job, and I have to say he was a dream employee. He brings a feeling of family-focused fun with a greater vision for everyone he works with.

I remember the first time Xavier and I worked together—I wanted a new eye-catching ad for the Ionic Breeze. Xavier had his headphones on and was listening to music and working on ads when I leaned over his shoulder to discuss some of my ideas. He brought them to life with accuracy and speed. From that day on, he became a go-to designer and had a huge impact on building and shaping the evolution of the brand. His work influenced the success of The Sharper Image catalogues and our retail store graphics. Xavier's genius is represented in three decades of striking cover designs, cutting edge photography art direction, and the drive to always push the envelope.

As my career has evolved, Xavier continues to meet my high expectations and be a creative force in all my endeavors, whether it be books, catalogs, product videos, web design, photography, or creating unique packaging for Sharper Image Design and RichardSolo products. We share similar creative aspirations, taste, and a passion for excellence. He's truly a creative genius.

Xavier, you are a pioneer. Thank you for your friendship, your family-focused good nature, and your amazing work. Your talent helped make The Sharper Image iconic and has impacted the major brand advertising trends we see today.

Thank you for your rich creative mind that so accurately reflects my imagination of invention.

Thank you for bringing these visions to life,

Richard

Dedicated to my father, Alan Thalheimer, who has helped me throughout my career. He has been my mentor, sounding board, confidant, advisor, and friend.

He has really been there and helped me through the difficult times. The Sharper Image would not have grown into this amazing retail phenomenon without the many hours of conversations between us.

And I must include my mother in this dedication. She taught me to be a perfectionist, along with an excellent level of taste and judgement in projects and products. She had a natural manner of making friends and making people feel appreciated, and she passed that wonderful quality along to me.

Thanks, Mom and Dad!

INTRODUCTION

I'm Richard Thalheimer, founder and former CEO of The Sharper Image. Since I started the company more than four decades ago, I've enjoyed being an entrepreneur and a CEO, and seeing how a business grows. That's why I want to share thoughts that can help you grow your business and make your business reflect your values. These are practical ideas that you can use every day and in almost every business situation.

The problems and solutions in this book are the situations that all of us deal with, regardless of company type. Sometimes we develop our solutions on the spot, and, over the years, we learn what works best for us. You've probably already run into problems relating to hiring, supervising, marketing, technology, cash flow, and all the challenges that come up every day.

These are the kinds of ideas I'll discuss in this book. Some of these ideas and principles will apply to you more than others, and you'll need to modify some of the advice to fit your particular business.

If you have a different point of view, or you disagree, that's fine, too. You wouldn't be in business for yourself or doing your own thing if you didn't have independent ideas and weren't a confident thinker. Entrepreneurs see things differently, and that's the way it should be. Take what you want, discard the rest. Surely, you'll find a few good ideas here that will help you. Here is your starting point!

Along with business ideas, the book will bring you up to date with all that has happened since 2004, when I released my first book, *Creating Your Own Sharper Image*. This 2020 book brings you everything I've experienced and learned since then, including the full story of what really happened when I was fired from The Sharper Image.

So much technology has changed in the 16 years between books. But despite all of this transformation, many things have remained the same—the business techniques mentioned in the following chapters. Maybe more than ever, you still need to find good people, motivate them to succeed, deal with your vendors, productively negotiate, get through the good times and the bad, and more. Human interaction techniques and personal motivation skills are still as important as the day I sat down to write my first book.

CHAPTER ONE

MY LIFETIME "JOB" STARTED AT 23

The year after graduating from Yale in 1970, I decided to move to San Francisco to start a business. So there I was, in my Volkswagen on Route 66, heading across the great Southwest. I didn't yet know exactly what I wanted to do, but I had spent a summer selling office supplies, copier paper, and toner. I was able to secure a wholesale source of these supplies in San Francisco, and I knew how to knock on doors.

I reached San Francisco at eight o'clock in the morning. Luckily, I found my way to Pacific Heights, one of the nicest neighborhoods in the city, and I responded to a "for rent" sign on a telephone pole. I signed the apartment lease that very afternoon, unpacked my things, and the next morning I headed down to the Financial District to start knocking on doors.

So, now I'm selling paper and toner, introducing myself to office purchasing managers, and learning how to sell directly. I had a small business, making deliveries in the morning, calling on offices in the afternoon, and typing invoices at night on my kitchen table. That was fine, but I wanted a much bigger business someday, so I went to law school to learn about contracts and business.

Law school didn't leave me much time to call on my customers directly, so I sent out mail-order circulars. That worked pretty well to generate orders and leverage my time, so I expanded to mailing them around the country and shipping orders. And I'm thinking, *wow, this is exciting—I'm learning the direct response mail order business!*

I liked the idea that you can mail out an offering to thousands of people or even millions once you get the formula right. (Of course, "mailed" might not necessarily apply today, replaced by online advertisement, or direct response on radio or television.)

Then an interesting thing happened. I was in a running club, and everybody wanted one of the new Seiko chronograph stopwatches that you could wear on your wrist. They could compute time, repel water, and take the sweat. In 1977, they cost about $300, but at the

Consumer Electronics Show in Las Vegas, I found an importer who had come up with a version I could afford to sell for $69. I knew right away; this was a great value, and I jumped on it.

THE DISCOVERY OF THE
RUNNER'S WATCH, AND MORE

I'd been reading *Runner's World* magazine, and I already knew that runners would want this watch, so I'm thinking, *why don't I do a full-page ad in Runner's World magazine for this watch?* My office supply business had sort of taught me how to sell things. So, I wrote the ad myself. It was a fun ad, and as soon as it appeared, thousands of orders were coming in. By the end of the year, I had made about $3 million selling this one watch, and in just a few magazines. By then, I had finished law school, and I was practicing law a bit, but the mail-order business was much more exciting to me than practicing law. I wanted to expand my mail-order advertising to lots of other magazines.

Then I thought, *"Why don't I find another product?"* So I combed the Consumer Electronics Show for more products, often those that big retailers overlooked. I introduced the first cordless telephone, which was, of course, very successful. Now it's hard to recall a time

FINALLY, A CHRONOGRAPH THAT KEEPS UP WITH AMAZING WALT STACK..

Walt Stack is an incredible man. He began running when he was 58. He is now 70 and has run 76 marathons, 9 fifty mile runs, and 1 one-hundred mile run. Each morning he bicycles 10 miles, runs 17 miles across the Golden Gate Bridge to Sausalito and back, jumps in the 50° salt water of the Bay for a half hour swim, then takes a half hour sauna at 200°. During all this morning activity he never takes off his Realtime Chronograph.

The Realtime Quartz Chronograph dramatically outdistances all watches in style, dependability and price. It was designed for active, athletic people like Walt, and now is available by mail from The Sharper Image for only $69 with ALL the following features.

MINIATURE TIME COMPUTER

In watch mode, it continually displays the hours, minutes, and seconds in large, easy to read liquid crystal numbers—without pressing buttons—even in direct sun.

The month, date and day of the week are immediately displayed with a touch of the side button. A night light is built in. The computer chip automatically adjusts for month end.

The Realtime weighs only 2.9 oz. with its stainless steel band or 1.5 oz. with a nylon band (not included). It has all the features you'll ever need in a watch or stopwatch, and is well protected by a slim stainless steel case.

TIME YOURSELF AND OTHERS

Record cumulative lap times. Splits. Switch to time of day and back. Take time out. And time beyond 60 minutes with automatic startover.

The stopwatch doesn't interfere with watch operation. Its quartz crystal vibrations split every second into 32,768 parts, making the Real-time more accurate than the finest mechanical chronograph ever made. You can time any event with precision to 1/100 of a second.

ACCURATE AND DURABLE

Unlike cheaper chronographs for the mass market, the Realtime Chronograph was built for rugged use. You can run and swim with it and not worry. If it can take

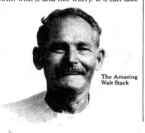

The Amazing
Walt Stack

the salt water of Walt's swimming, your perspiration won't harm it. It's water resistant down to 80 feet below the surface. The Realtime case and band are 100% stainless steel, not base metal or plastic. The face crystal is hard, scratch resistant rock glass, not plastic.

Accuracy is within 65 seconds a year. Its Union Carbide batteries last a year or more (unlike LED'S) and can easily be changed by your jeweler. Separate battery for night light gives you extra dependability and longer life.

MAINTENANCE FREE

Your Realtime has no moving parts and will probably never need service even after years of hard use. It carries a one year factory warranty on parts and labor. In the unlikely event it needs repair, prompt service by mail facilities are right here in the U.S.

ORDER WITHOUT OBLIGATION

We want you to be satisfied with your Realtime Chronograph. After you receive it, wear it. Compare it with any other chronograph. If for any reason it's not what you expected, return it within two weeks. You're guaranteed a full and courteous refund, with no questions asked.

15

when we had never heard of a cordless phone. My next releases were the first car radar detector, then the first home answering machine, followed by a host of others. Some magazine ads did better than others, but they all made money.

It was 1979, long before the Internet showed up. I had built up a customer list, and I could find more new products, so, I thought, *"Well, why don't I try a color catalog, grouping these products?"* That year, the first Sharper Image catalog went out. I put every penny I had into that mailing.

If it hadn't been successful, I would probably have gone out of business right then. But I knew my market, and I knew my products. I made a calculated estimate that there was no way I would lose any money, so I had the odds in my favor as I sent out that catalog. It worked. The catalog brought in more gross profit than the expense to mail it.

THE FIRST STORE LEADS TO MANY MORE

Customers were coming up to the office all the time, trying to buy these products. In 1981, I thought, *"Why don't we open a store, so these people have someplace to buy?"* Even though the store location I chose was in a quiet neighborhood of downtown San Francisco, it did a lot of sales, right from the beginning. The catalog mailings brought in customers in droves.

Well, fast-forward about three decades from there, and there were about 180 Sharper Image stores, and the business was beginning to approach a billion dollars. We were also enjoying a fantastic $100-million-plus Internet business, as well as the incredibly successful mail-order catalog. There were lots of ups and downs along the way, but it finally was really working!

By the year 2000, things got better and better because we learned over the years what worked and what didn't. That's what I want to share with you: what has worked, and what I have learned from this school of hard knocks.

There's a sort of joke that Mother Nature gives the experience before she gives the lesson. That's certainly been my experience. I wish I had known the lesson before I got the experience. But after all these years, I've learned a lot, and that's what I'm going to share with you.

DEFINING THE MISSION: THE SHARPER IMAGE FOR EVERYONE

I first defined the mission of The Sharper Image as: "To share the fun of discovering products that make life easier and more enjoyable." When we first started, though, most of the products we discovered were for male executives, sort of boys' toys. As the years went by, we adapted into a different type of business model.

Instead of just selling suits of armor, James Bond crossbows, or Motorized Massage Chairs, the slogan became *"Sharper Image for Everyone"* because we sold a range of products that were useful for women, too. Whether it was a nose-and-ear-hair trimmer, an air purifier, a hair dryer that also conditions hair, the first piece of Nautilus exercise equipment for the home, the world's first automatic eyeglasses cleaner, or a music product with a Sound Soother environmental sound library, our products evolved to cover a broader demographic. Price points ranged from $10 to several thousand dollars, with many products going for $30, $50, or $100.

Given our expanded demographic and focus on attractively priced fun and functional products, we could open stores in almost any location. The catalog and website helped to attract store visitors. These changes allowed the business to grow from its humble beginnings to a $750 million business at its peak. It became a very different business than the one you may have seen in the 1980s.

As I'll talk about more in this book, all businesses continue to evolve. I anticipated that fact when I came up with the name *The Sharper Image*. I wanted something that would let the business expand into new areas rather than limiting it.

WHAT'S IN A NAME? A *LOT.*

When I first arrived in San Francisco's Financial District to sell paper, I needed a name for my business. Because I was required by law to register my business, I used my own name because it is more difficult to register a fictitious name. You may notice, however, that Thalheimer Paper Systems does not exactly roll off the tongue.

I love business names that sound good and are easy to read, pronounce, spell, and remember. A name like that is a great asset to any starting business. Some of my favorites are Apple, Amazon, Land Rover, Starbucks, Home Depot, Facebook, Uber, Tiffany, Chipotle, Shopify, Domino's, Twitter, Zoom, and Tesla.

On the other hand, names that *don't* roll off the tongue make your potential customer work a lot harder, and they can be hard to find on the Internet. For example, the name Hammacher Schlemmer, the famous catalog company, is a tough Google Search. Does it have a hyphen? Are there four m's or just three? We can remember and pronounce Gucci, but names like Yves Saint Laurent, Altria, or Hyundai don't easily stick in the brain.

So, I knew my first business name would have to be replaced eventually. One day, *The Sharper Image* popped into my mind. It would work for the business I had, and the business I wanted it to be. I knew it would let me sell anything someday.

I knew I had found a catchy, solid name, so I wouldn't give it up when, a few years later, my first creative director asked if I would consider changing it. He said it was too long and difficult to fit into advertising copy placements. By then, I really liked the name, and wouldn't consider changing it. He was a brilliant creative director who helped me enormously, but I knew my customers and my image, so I held firm.

From that experience, I learned the importance of trusting your own instincts, sometimes even in the face of contradictory advice from an expert. It's your business, and you know it best.

Over the years, The Sharper Image sold everything imaginable: a two-person submarine, customized Harley Davidson motorcycles, a knight's suit of armor, autographed music sheets from The Beatles, original art from Peter Max, restored collectible cars, and many more interesting and unique items. The name The Sharper Image enabled that variety, and covered all those products.

CHAPTER TWO

BUILD SOMETHING ORIGINAL

f there is one thing I want to emphasize, it is that originality is the key to success.

There are examples of successful businesses that copied another's idea and did it successfully; for example, Lyft copied Uber, and they are both doing well. However, this shows the first market mover advantage, and the first to market often enjoys bigger and better success. Tesla is the best example of that, completely capturing the luxury electric vehicle market despite competition from Audi, VW, Porsche, Jaguar, and others. Whether they will keep that leadership in 10 or 20 years from now remains to be seen, but the race is theirs to lose at this moment. Being original and the first-mover are powerful advantages. Apple was the first mover in smartphones; Starbucks in coffee; Nike in modern running shoes; Zoom in teleconferencing.

WHAT'S IN *YOUR* BUSINESS NAME?

For your endeavor, you may prefer a name that tells people exactly what you're doing. For example, Hans German Motors, Home Computer Solutions, or Bruno's Little Italy might do well if you want to communicate a purpose or a service.

Being specific, though, doesn't mean you can't be original. Maybe Precision German Motors or Efficient Home Computer Solutions would be a better twist on the same idea. Get the benefit right in the headline if you can. Your business name *is* a headline, and your website address needs to reflect it. Make it work for you as much as it can.

Of course, you want to be proud of the name of your business. You're going to sell it to others, you'll ask them for business, and you'll be using this name for a long time. Put a lot of thought into it, and it will serve you well.

REGISTER YOUR BUSINESS
NAME AS A DOMAIN

After you decide on your business name, go on a web domain registering site like Network Solutions or GoDaddy, and find out if that name is available, and with what suffix. Most, but not all, web businesses have a .com as their suffix. It's preferred *because* it's the most common, so it's easy to remember.

When you type in your desired name and see if it is available, also see how it looks in print. Some names are easier to read than others. The juxtaposition of vowels and consonants makes a difference in readability also. Eventually, you should find a name that both resonates with you and is available. It doesn't cost much to register a name, so you might want to register it right away, even if you want to keep thinking about it.

Years ago, getting a name trade-marked was extremely important. Today, getting a name registered as a website domain is just as important.

PURSUE WHAT YOU LOVE

Some people work their entire life so they can eventually retire and stop working, while others want to work for-ever, retiring only because of health issues or company policies. Having an occupation that you love is probably the single most significant predictor of success. It is so much more fun to wake up in the morning with a genuine desire to go to work, and that attitude will make you so much better at your work. Your challenge is to find an area that stimulates and excites you.

If you've ever watched Suze Orman, the financial advisor, you can tell that she clearly enjoys giving financial advice on television. You see the same love of performing in Jimmy Fallon, Stephen Colbert, and other late-night show hosts.

That's the way I always felt about my job. I loved being a creator and buyer of products, thinking up new product ideas, or taking an existing product and figuring out how to make it better. The creative process satisfied and fulfilled me.

I loved both very different parts of it: finding the products and marketing them. I discovered a long time ago that it doesn't do any good to have the best idea in the world if you can't get it sold.

That runner's watch I told you about is a perfect example. I loved every minute of finding the product. As a runner, I also loved the product: You might even be able to imagine my excitement when I saw a comparable product that cost less than a quarter of the Seiko's price. I also loved every minute of selling it: Because I loved the product and selling in general, it was easy for me to write the ads from my heart.

People often say they want to make money, but that's not what a career or a business is really about. It's so much better to make money doing something you love. In fact, just doing something you love is what's more important. That's what allows you to do it night and day for a long time with that same excitement.

It can take years, even decades, to build your success. If you're going to work at something for that long, you had better love doing it. It's always struck me as sad when people fall into a career choice in college, go to graduate school, and get a job without ever deciding if they love that work. They might work hard because they need the income to support a family or build security, but there's no passion in the work. Fortunately, that doesn't apply to everyone. Some people do choose early on what they want to do, and they love it throughout their careers.

As I've made clear so far, I'm closer to that second category. Although, when I was young, I didn't know exactly what I wanted to do with my life, I've always felt the need and desire to be the boss in a business of my own. From my personal experience, it seems not so important to know exactly what you want to do at a young age. Maybe it'll work out better for you that way, too. However, what is essential is to keep looking until you find something you can throw yourself into without reservation.

One of my favorite late-bloomer-success stories is Harlan Sanders, who founded a chain of fast-food restaurants that is now called KFC. I grew up knowing it as Kentucky Fried Chicken, one of the first successful national fast-food franchises. But Colonel Sanders himself didn't become a success and found that chain until he was in his 60s. Until then, he had been living and sleeping in his car.

Sanders' story shows that it's never too late to build a big success, even at an age that many of us think of as retirement. Most importantly, he loved what he did, and he didn't stop until he made it a success.

YOUR BUSINESS SHOULD BE AS ORIGINAL AS YOU ARE

America has become such a sophisticated marketplace, and the Internet makes it so easy to compare prices on make and model of every product. If you can be distinctive in the market—not price-shopped for the same items elsewhere, you've got a big advantage. So many businesses are alike; yours must be different in a way to give you a marketing edge.

If your business is unique, it is less vulnerable to being knocked off by a bigger competitor. Make it as difficult for them as you can because more established players often copy startups. There were literally a dozen knock-off catalogs trying to copy what we were doing and how we looked. There were also stores in shopping malls designed to match the look and feel of ours. The Macy's department store in San Francisco even created an entire floor that looked just like The Sharper Image store, down to the products and even the fixtures. I was so discouraged by that.

If we were going to grow and prosper, we needed unique products and packaging, as we had when we started in the '80s. We had to *reinvent* ourselves. I decided the only way to be unique was to design and manufacture our own products. That meant coming up with product ideas, designing them, creating the steel tools that press the plastic parts, getting the patents, making the electronic circuits, and designing and doing the packaging.

That turned out to be one of the most difficult approaches I could have imagined. It takes a minimum of 20,000 units to justify manufacturing a product. Back then, we were barely able to sell a production run of 3,000 units, so we were sort of small to embark on this ambition. However, we were still growing a lot, adding stores and catalog mailings, so I took the risk that we could sell exclusive products in much higher volume.

In order to make these original products, we started thinking about how to modify or even create from scratch some new product ideas, and before long, we called our group "Sharper Image Design." Originally, the team consisted of our product lead manager, a product designer, a graphic designer for the boxes, a mechanical engineer, and an electrical engineer. Years later, we grew to about 12 people. We met twice weekly and batted around product ideas, looked at drawings, discussed product prototypes, and all the details involved in making products. We worked primarily with Chinese manufacturers. Of course, we preferred to build products in the US, but at the time, most manufacturing involving plastic molding and circuit board assembly was done in China. What a fun and productive time we had! It was one of the most enjoyable parts of my career because it involved being creative and seeing a project go from conception to a finished item on the shelf at a Sharper Image store.

In 1993, we made one of our most successful products, the "Motorized Tie Rack," which spins neckties around, hanging on your closet rod, at the press of a button. We also manufactured a new type of key ring that made it easier to organize and remove keys. Fortunately, they each eventually sold more than 50,000 units, becoming two of our best sellers. We went on to invent and make more than 200 different products, which our competitors couldn't touch. We had found a successful formula.

By 2004, about 80 percent of our sales were Sharper Image products that were exclusive to us—with our brand and our packaging. We invented and manufactured half of them under the Sharper Image Design name. The other products were made with The Sharper Image name, and we negotiated exclusive distribution. We had accomplished the goal of creating exclusive, special products, and created a business that was quite distinctive from others. That made it much more difficult for someone to copy us. Two decades of building a solid culture of product creation made it virtually impossible for a competitor to compete with us in our particular retail area.

This idea works for you, too. No matter what your business' specialty is, make it unique. When you do, you'll find it easier to maintain your pricing, hold on to your customers, and build long-term loyalty. Your business's special characteristics can be made up of many parts, starting with the name and the logo. If you advertise, consider a unique slogan, music, or graphic. Make it memorable, catchy, and use it consistently. If you manufacture products, they should be unique or modified enough in feature or color or appearance to differentiate them from your competition. Your physical place of business might look unusual, or your staff might wear unique clothing or accessories.

For example, when I visit the Tesla sales or service center, everyone is wearing Tesla logo shirts or jackets. Same at the Apple store. It looks really sharp. I am impressed.

SUCCESS IS 1% INSPIRATION
AND 99% PERSPIRATION

Thomas Edison, who invented among others, the early light bulb, motion pictures, sound recording, and the phonograph, was one of the most inspired inventors of all time, yet he valued hard work more. As he famously said, "Success is 1% inspiration and 99% perspiration," meaning that the effort and the follow-through are more important than the idea.

That's been my experience as well. I can't even count the number of people who have said to me, "You know, I had an idea to start a business like The Sharper Image. I should have followed up on it." Or, "I had this great product idea. I could have been rich if I'd gotten it to market." When I hear this, I sort of inwardly shrug and think, "You don't realize that having a good idea is only the beginning."

Most of the variables leading to success are not the ideas, not wishes, or dreams, but being committed to making it happen. The actual work of creating success is a lot harder than the idea. You need to just get started and keep moving in a positive direction. I realize it can be hard to get something done each day, but that's precisely what you need to do. Every day, I would ask myself, "What have I done today, not just to maintain what I have but also to move things forward into a new and bigger future?"

Every day, do *something*, no matter how small, to make things move forward towards a more successful tomorrow. Overcome the too-easy temptation to make excuses why today is not the day. Push through the difficulty of maintaining your motivation month after month and year after year. You can do it, and you will succeed. That's the mindset of an entrepreneur.

START SMALL AND FINISH BIG

Have you dreamed of launching a big, well-financed, venture capital startup? That can certainly work, but it is not the "small step" approach I took. I built The Sharper Image, slowly, one brick at a time, so it didn't grow as quickly as other businesses. On the other hand, because I built it slowly and carefully, it was more solid than many companies.

Speaking of taking small steps to get started, how small is too small a step? No step is too small when you're starting. The most challenging thing about starting any new project is getting it off the ground. For me, it's worked well to break every objective, every goal, down into smaller and smaller steps until the first step is one that I can actually start and accomplish.

Remember the Bill Murray movie *What About Bob?* In this movie, the title character is a neurotic patient, who tries to follow his psychiatrist's advice. When he first comes in for therapy, he's too frightened and anxious to accomplish anything on his own. Eventually, he learns the value of taking baby steps.

That's good advice for business owners, too: Take baby steps. That first step may be as simple as making a phone call and asking about the availability of a product or a service. If you learn it isn't available, that could be good news. Perhaps *you* could offer it. Or perhaps it *is* available, and the prices are much higher than you expected. That could give you an opportunity to find it at a lower cost, as I did with the watch. If you learn that the customer relations of that product are terrible, there's your chance to start something better. Making a phone call, or sending an email and asking some questions takes nothing but your time. From those questions, you'll probably figure out the next step that you want to make. Once you figure out the first step, then you'll probably see the second step, and so on.

Of course, you eventually want to get to a goal. These baby steps have to lead somewhere, hopefully to your vision of success. This analogy works in a lot of situations.

You may have run a marathon or known someone that did. A great technique for running these long races is to start slow and accelerate throughout the race. The worst thing you can do is to sprint out of the start and then fade and limp along, barely making it to the end. Business and life are the same way. It is a winning formula to start slow and finish strong.

ENTREPRENEURS ARE OPTIMISTS

You really can't be an entrepreneur unless you're optimistic. That's because every entrepreneur encounters so much negative energy and so much adversity when they start out, that if they weren't an optimist, they would probably never continue.

What's an optimist? One way to define it is someone who sees the glass half full rather than half empty. I'm always looking at that half-full glass and saying, "Here's how we could fill it up."

Expect other people to give you a hard time and tell you in great detail why something won't work. This never fails to amaze me. People with backgrounds in finance or accounting are especially likely to discourage you and tell you why it can't be done.

When I decided that we should go into designing, creating, and manufacturing our own products, so many people told me it was a recipe for disaster. Of course, they'd feel that way. Who would think that a retailer could do all that? Yet 10 years later, it turned out to be the key to our success. Our products were different from everyone else's. They had better margins, and they made The Sharper Image unique, so it worked out perfectly. There were so many objections along the way. If I had listened to them all, we would have never gone forward. One of my favorite sayings is, "If all objections must be overcome, nothing will ever be accomplished," and I believe it with all my heart.

Now, don't get me wrong. There are plenty of people who fail because they work in the "wrong order." They sort of go "ready, fire, aim," which is probably not going to work. You need a plan, and you need to carry it out accurately. But that's different from planning so long and so thoroughly that nothing ever gets started, much less ever gets finished.

I remember a senior merchandise manager who worked for me. He came highly recommended, and he seemed to have the qualifications to supervise the selection of products. However, he had a difficult time getting started on any project. We would discuss the project, then he would go to his office, pull out his legal pad, and start analyzing and writing and strategizing.

I'd drop in his office a day or two later, and he'd still be writing on his legal pad. And I thought to myself, *"You've got to get started."* He never took the first step. There was no baby step; there was just his writing on a legal pad. We parted ways after only a month, and I thought, *"This is so the opposite of the way I am."*

You can't just keep doodling forever. You've got to do something to take action. And the sooner you take action and get started, the sooner you can see if you are on the right track, and if not, rethink your strategy. I call it a "sense of urgency," and mine is much higher than most people's. I also see it in successful managers. Their sense of urgency to get things done is so vital to the overall result. When you combine the optimistic view that says, "Things can be done," with a sense of urgency to take a step today to make things happen, you've got a powerful combination of factors carrying you toward your goal.

HOT WATER AND BATHTUB VISIONS

When I began selling office supplies door to door, I often wondered where it might lead and how I would get there. One technique worked really well for me. Perhaps some version of it will work for you, too. My apartment didn't have a shower, oddly enough, but it had a great bathtub. After a hard day at work, I would take long baths, and while sitting in the hot water, I would let my mind wander. I would think about two things. One, "Where am I now in my business?" and two, "Where do I want to be a year, five years, or 10 years from now?"

In the "present," I was knocking on doors in the financial district of San Francisco selling copier supplies. In 10 years, I wanted a large company selling a variety of products all over the country. The next obvious thing to figure out was, "How do I get from here to there?"

You could call it daydreaming, but that's the only way to do this. I really believe that only when you visualize your dreams can you actually reach them. You need the fantasy and the vision of where you want to go to have much hope of getting there. Don't let anyone discourage you from visualizing a terrific success down the road. Your fantasies will more likely become a reality once you know what they are, and once you start working on the first steps to get there.

Since I moved from that apartment, I haven't had a bathtub like that one. I have found that long, solitary walks are a great substitute, probably even better because you get some exercise while you're daydreaming. Long bike rides work well, too. Whatever gives you time to reflect, to analyze, and to daydream is a really important part of your planning, so don't ever think that daydreaming is a waste of time. That is certainly not true. Visualizing your fantasies is one of the most meaningful steps to reaching your goals.

HAVE YOU SET YOUR SIGHTS TOO LOW?

When I started my business, my short- and interme-
diate-term goals evolved, but I never stopped fanta-
sizing about my long-term goal of having a really large
company. I might plan just to double business revenues
during the coming year. I would devise specific steps for
reaching that goal. For example, I might mail out twice as
many catalogs.

Some years, my goals were less ambitious, like keeping the business at the same level or growing by 20 percent. The point is, you need to set goals that are ambitious enough so that when you meet them, you're moving
along at a growth pace that's eventually taking you to
where you want to be. You don't want to work hard for
20 years but end up with a successful small business that
can't support your life's needs.

Ask yourself, "Even if I am successful in my short-
er-term goals, where does that put me in five years or 10
years?" Will it be enough, or is it really a lower level of
income and success than I need to live? It's a balancing
act. You want to set goals that aren't so high you can't
reach them; while on the other hand, setting them high
enough so that when you reach them, you're where you
want to be. Sometimes, that requires us to switch careers
altogether. Of course, I appreciate and understand that

sometimes a fulfilling career may not be very well-compensated, but it may provide great soul satisfaction. That is a wonderful life, too.

The first profession you enter might not satisfy you. Perhaps you thought you would enjoy the work but then found out you didn't. Or perhaps, down the road, you realized your chosen field wasn't going to provide the level of income that you need. Or maybe you're working for a company that isn't recognizing your talents and promoting you, and you need to change jobs, careers, or companies.

People become dissatisfied for a variety of reasons, and it's perfectly normal. Dissatisfaction can be a positive influence and a positive driver for you to reach your life goals. You should continuously reevaluate your situation and ask yourself, "Am I pleased with the progress I'm making?" If your answer is no, start thinking about how to change it, so you can be fully engaged and satisfied with what you're doing and where it's taking you.

CHAPTER THREE

HOW TO WIN CUSTOMERS

YOUR BUSINESS WILL SUCCEED IF YOU ATTRACT AND KEEP CUSTOMERS

am always fascinated that some restaurants open and have immediate success with lots of customers, and others struggle to keep a clientele. It might be the quality of the food, but sometimes it just comes down to attracting and keeping customers.

That is one, if not the most important, aspect of any enterprise. Rarely, a product or service is so desirable that customer service is not determinative of success.

But usually, winning customers is of utmost importance. You have probably experienced this in your own life. Don't you go back to places or services that give you great customer service? I certainly do. Let's talk about building positive customer interactions.

PERFECT YOUR BUSINESS GREETING

Whether you're on a sales floor, making a sales call to the office manager, or starring in a television news show or infomercial, how you greet people matters. Your greeting should include genuine eye contact. Look directly into the person's eyes or camera lens and don't look away. Shifting eyes *look* shifty. Of course, you also don't want to stare so obsessively that it is creepy. Make it a good balance.

Accompany your gaze with a warm smile. Say hello in a tone of voice that nonverbally conveys to the other person, *I feel great, I'm a warm and likable human being, and I like being here to greet you. I'm conveying an emotion of interest and warmth to let you know that I'm actually enthusiastic to be here helping you.*

If that seems a bit over the top for your personality, maybe you can tone it down to fit, but trust me, most people will respond more positively to someone who is warm and enthusiastic. It's hard to make a sale when the customer perceives you as aloof, cold, or distant.

Some years ago, I walked into the local Porsche automobile dealership where I had purchased two cars over about 10 years. On this particular day, though, no one recognized or greeted me. I had never before seen the salesperson on duty, sort of a gruff, crusty type. He didn't get up from his desk or even acknowledge my presence. Instead, he shot me a cursory glance and finally issued a curt offer of help. His unfriendly tone made me certain I didn't want any help from him, so I left the dealership and didn't return for about a year.

During that time, I enjoyed telling the story and told it a lot, resulting in some bad word-of-mouth every time. After that year, I returned to the dealership. This time, I was greeted warmly and enthusiastically by the person who had sold me a Porsche years before. What a difference! It totally turned me around and made me want to buy from them again.

Sharper Image salespeople have always been trained to greet everyone with enthusiasm. Some do it better than others because perhaps the others are a bit shy, not "people persons." We try to hire salespeople who are outgoing, warm, and enthusiastic, but sometimes we get the other type. However, unless they find a genuine warmth in their personality, I can bet you they won't achieve the sales results they need to, and they probably won't make it in the long-term. That's just the way it is in sales.

You must make the other person want to do business with you. That's true even for a business that doesn't involve direct sales. Whether it's a restaurant, a broker-age firm, or something else, almost every business needs to convince others of the desirability of seeing him or her again in a professional context. Almost every business has customers, and every customer wants to feel wanted and treated well.

Think about that for a moment. Whether you're talking with your doctor or lawyer or acupuncturist or house painter, you don't need to spend your hard-earned money on any of them when you have other choices. To a certain extent, they're selling you on having confidence that you want to do business with them, not the others. Business is about relationships. We are all looking to be treated well in our relationships, and business is no exception.

CUSTOMER RELATIONS IN THREE EASY STEPS

One big advantage I have in business is being secure enough to say when I mess up. That may sound easy, but a lot of people cannot admit they made a mistake. No doubt you've needed to complain to a store or a business about a problem, and you would appreciate it so much if they would just tell you how sorry they are that they screwed up. But if instead, the person you're talking to gets defensive, you get frustrated, and you probably won't do business with them again.

This happens all the time. The defensive store clerk or store manager blames it on something else. It's the computer's fault, or they didn't make the reservation, or another excuse. That's the *worst* possible response.

"Any business can take an order well, but only a great business can handle a problem well." Why not use simple approaches to customer relations that work, make everyone happy, and bring the customer back again? Here is the easiest business approach to customer relations ever, which takes the upset customer and turns the situation into a positive one.

What to do when you're confronted with an angry customer:

1. First, admit you made a mistake and apologize sincerely for the problem. Repeat what the customer just complained about because it shows you heard them.

2. Ask the customer what they'd like you to do to fix the situation. After all, what the customer *thinks* they want is usually what they actually want. It's a common mistake to instead try to give them what you want. In your suggested course of action, try to incorporate elements of what they are asking.

3. Promptly take action to show the customer you are genuinely attempting to solve the problem, or at least improve the situation. If at all possible, give the customer more than they asked for.

If you do give the customer more than they expect, they will probably tell their friends, "I can't believe The Sharper Image did this for me! They gave me a new unit!" (or "exchanged it so quickly," or whatever). They might say, "I went into The Sharper Image, I had this problem, and they took care of it right away. Can you believe a business would treat you that well?" That's exactly the positive word-of-mouth you want to have circulated about your business. It's worth so many more times over what it cost to create.

What about the situation that was actually the customer's mistake, and not yours? Should you still apologize and try to make it right? Definitely! The customer doesn't see it as their mistake. They wouldn't have brought it up unless they felt they had been wronged somehow. Anyway, it really is not about who is right or who is wrong. It's about making the customer feel that you have a responsive business that's catering to him or her right then, on their terms.

Your mission is not to convince the customer that they're wrong. It's to make them want to buy from your business again and again. The surest way to do it is to make them understand that your company listens and responds to the customer.

If you positively cannot afford to give them what they want, and it really is not your fault in any way, do a modification of this approach: Give lip service to the apology, describe your intention to make it right, and then make whatever offer you *can* make while describing it to them in the most positive terms possible. That's a pragmatic approach, and once in a while, that's what you may have to do.

View every customer problem as an opportunity to show what a great business you have and to leave the customer feeling that they want to do business with you in the future. Keep in mind this simple but important fact: it is always less expensive to keep an existing customer than it is to pay the price to acquire a new customer. In fact, a new customer costs you five times as much. It costs so much less to accommodate a reasonable request or an almost reasonable request by the current customer. So bend over backward, be accommodating, and keep that customer happy!

CLASSIC SELLING TECHNIQUES
THAT ACTUALLY WORK

When I wrote my first book in 2004, most selling took place in person. Telephone conversations were good, but personal meetings were always better. Today, many sales transactions occur digitally, by clicks, bidding, email, text, or video conference. The classic sales-closing techniques can still be useful, however. Timeless techniques never go away, though they certainly evolve.

Every experienced and professional salesperson uses these easy-to-learn closing techniques. If you don't know them yet, you'll find they can really help you. Let me demonstrate them through this scenario:

Imagine that the sales rep is having some sort of conversation with a prospective customer about a potential deal or purchase. It might be in a retail store, in the person's home or office, or in a phone conversation. Now the customer has stopped talking, and the moment has arrived. The sales rep needs to do one very important thing: They need to ask a question that is deliberately designed to lead to a close.

Let me give you some examples: "Jim, do you think you'd like to get the red one or the blue one?" Giving the prospect a choice is one of the simplest closing techniques possible. "Would you like to get the small or the medium? Do you prefer real leather or synthetic? 256K or 512K?"

Take a look at some more examples. "Mrs. Purchasing Agent, do you want to set up the contract to get the automatic delivery with the discount that I mentioned?

Or do you prefer to order as you need replenishment?" Or, "Carolyn, do you want to move forward now, and I'll start with setting up the incentive program for your sales staff? Or do you want to discuss the alternatives with your team first, and I'll check back next week?" Or, "Chuck, how many units work for you as a first order?" or "Alexandria, is that price good enough that we can place your order today?"

As you can see, every one of these questions requires a response from the prospective buyer, and every one of them heads toward a close. Ask the question, then stop talking. A moment of silence is okay; let the seconds tick by. Give the other person time to answer. When they do, listen carefully.

If the answer is not an immediate agreement to complete the transaction, be prepared to acknowledge their objection. Then ask the next question, "All right, that makes sense. How about if I call you in two weeks and see if you're ready to place your order then?" Or you might say, "Bob, I'm disappointed this deal still hasn't tempted you. Is it okay if I sleep on this, and call you in two days, and I'll do some research to see if it's possible to give you a better deal?" Or, "Jack, since you've said it's premature to set up the new incentive program now, is it okay with you if I work on this, and come back with some further thoughts to improve the program?

I'd like to come back next week and show you the refinements. Would that be okay, maybe after Wednesday next week?"

By responding this way, you're doing two things. One, you're avoiding taking "no" for an answer. Instead, you're shifting towards a future opportunity to make the close. Two, and most importantly, you're keeping the relationship alive and healthy. It's not ending; it's just momentarily postponed. There is a big difference; inexperienced reps often take the first no as final, but you don't really want that to be the end.

Successful salespeople practice the technique I just mentioned all the time. If you're just starting out, it might take you a bit more effort at first, but it will become second nature. Attempt to close, don't take "no" for an answer, leave yourself an out, and make a commitment for a future conversation. Most sales closings happen after a series of "nos." Typically, a salesperson hears three of them before closing the sale. It is a well-known truism that the salesperson's job begins after the "no."

HOW LONG DO YOU WANT TO KEEP A CUSTOMER?

Each new customer acquisition is expensive and definitely a lot more costly than getting a customer to repeat and buy again. There are a few transactions that are "one time;" typically that would be selling your house for example. You won't probably sell another house to that buyer again.

For most businesses, though, perhaps a fast-food franchise like Chipotle, repeat customers are essential. You need that customer to return again and again, year after year. That was certainly true of The Sharper Image. I wanted customers to come back at least once, maybe twice a year, sometimes a lot more, and for many years to come. Many loyal customers continued to buy from us for 20 years or more. Part of the reason was that we treated them so well. Some years we may have had a lot of products they wanted, maybe fewer another year, but those customers always appreciated our courtesy, respectful treatment, return privileges, and perhaps help with a repair or a refund.

As a result, there were only a few past customers who weren't willing to come back to The Sharper Image. Because of our great interactions with them, most customers continued to see what was new.

Treat your customers as if you want them to come back again and again for 20 or 40 years. To do that, remember the lesson I told you before: The customer always thinks they're right. Your job is never to convince them otherwise. It's to make them want to come back.

TREAT EVERYONE WITH RESPECT

In case I didn't already make it clear, I strongly believe that good manners and politeness make a lot of difference in the long-term success or failure of your business, and they cost nothing. What a great impression they make on your customers and your business! Magic words, like "please" or "thank you," and "yes, ma'am" or "yes, sir," are absolutely guaranteed to win you friends and customer loyalty. And always remember to use the words "yes" or "yes, sir" instead of the slang, "uh-huh" or "OK."

Imagine the customer calls to ask whether a particular item is in stock, and the sales rep says, "Yes, sir, we have both models in stock. Would you like me to hold one for you?" Now compare that with this response, "Yeah, we've got some," or even, "Uh-huh." Which sounds better to you? The second style may be fine for teenagers in a clothing chain but not for a national business for grownups. The nice thing about good manners is that the customers who appreciate it will really appreciate it, and the ones who don't notice won't mind them at all.

In fact, treat *everyone* with respect, whether they're a customer or not. That includes the receptionist on the phone, the counter help at your local fast-food takeout place, and the plumber. The effort to charm everyone you

meet will not only make you popular and give you practice for dealing with your own customers, but it may provide additional rewards. For one thing, you'll feel good
seeing how happy you can make others. It's a great way
to go through the day. What's more, when you want to
get an entrée into a particular office or you need a favor
from someone, your charm might make all the difference.

In someone else's store the other day, I asked the store
manager to make an exception on a product exchange,
which she didn't want to do. I replied, "You know, I completely understand. You're doing your job, and you're
doing it well. You're following the company policy. Who
can I contact who has the authority to make this exception? Would you give me their name and phone number?"

I was combining politeness and respect with my
request to speak to someone in authority and that did the
trick. I don't know if her pride made her want to prove
to me that she had the authority, or she didn't want her
boss to get a complaint about her store, but she suddenly
decided to do what I asked. I thanked her profusely, and I
told her I was going to write to the head of the company
about what a terrific manager she is.

You can definitely catch more flies with honey than
vinegar. Try it tomorrow: Be charming to everyone you
run into. You'll probably have a lot of fun, even when
you're being critical when you do it with respect.

TREAT YOUR SUPPLIERS LIKE
YOUR CUSTOMERS

Your suppliers are just as important to your future as your customers. After all, they provide the inventory and support services that keep your business going, so keep them happy. *This is not always as obvious as it should be.*

Over the years, I have been surprised when I observed our merchandise buyers sometimes treating vendors with a forceful or disrespectful tone. I occasionally saw a buyer pressuring a vendor, or burdening them with an unnecessary expense or inconvenience because they felt the vendor's role as subservient to their position.

For a moment, it may feel that you are powerful if you are tough on vendors, or that you will only "win" the negotiation by asking for even more than you really need.

This relationship dynamic can be easy to fall into, especially if you're early in your career. It is crucial that you treat suppliers with respect. As I continued to see this type of interaction over the years, I quickly began to recognize it and saw that the buyers honestly thought they were doing a good job for The Sharper Image.

One of the most important pieces of advice I can share with you is about respecting everyone, at every level in every area of your business. We need to see the big picture. Product buyers need their vendors to support them. Remember, word-of-mouth circulates among your supplier and support community. You need it to be positive. You want dedicated loyalty from your suppliers, so they'll come to your aid when you need it.

During the difficult recession of 1990, some of our major suppliers, like Sony and Panasonic, cut back on our available credit, even though we were doing fine. They had gotten burned by some larger department stores declaring bankruptcy, so they were very afraid it might spread to other retailers.

Because they weren't very loyal suppliers, they made our life a lot more difficult than it needed to be. The medium and smaller suppliers, on the other hand, were so steadfast and they did everything they could to help us get through that difficult year. For example, at our request, they looked through their costs and passed along savings where possible. Just because we asked, they also extended our credit terms during the Christmas season from 30-day terms to 60 or 90 days. This really helped us get by, at a time of year when the extra inventory and the payment terms were critical. And when times returned to normal, I remembered what happened. The big suppliers like Sony were cut back in our product ordering, and at my direction, we deliberately gave them less business; the smaller, more loyal suppliers were rewarded. Eventually, we were not selling any Sony products. I had made a determined effort to wean our company away from these suppliers that did not stand by us, and it proved to be a good decision. We did better without them, and of course, eventually making our own products.

Over the years, I trained our buyers to treat suppliers well and made this a key part of our culture at The Sharper Image. I want to pass that same thought along to you.

Smaller vendors need you as much as you need them. Never take advantage of any one of them, or ignore them, or treat them with less care because you feel you're in the power seat because you're paying them. Instead, treat them as well as you treat your customers, and continue to build and cultivate solid relationships to endure through the years. You never know, they might even end up working for your company someday!

ANY PUBLICITY IS GOOD PUBLICITY

I can't leave the chapter about winning customers without talking about how publicity can contribute to it. The famous promoter P.T. Barnum actually said, "Any publicity is good publicity so long as they spell your name right," and it's probably true with some limitations. It's useful to be noticed and commented upon, especially in the world of entertainment and music. So many performers and stars have seen their careers take off or come back after some outrageous piece of publicity. Consider the Janet Jackson incident at the 2004 Super Bowl. It got her a lot of attention, and her career benefitted.

The most famous recent example is Kim Kardashian. Years after soaring to fame based on some inappropriate sex tape video, she and her husband Kanye West remain in the spotlight. Not everyone admires the publicity that brought her to this point, but it's evident that it brought her fame, wealth, and connection.

Of course, really negative publicity, especially when connected to criminal behavior, is not the sort of publicity one would want. But in general, getting publicity for your business is a good thing. At The Sharper Image, we did a lot to cooperate with news television, entertainment television, and other programs that asked to come into our stores and report on them, especially around the holiday season.

I've been fortunate to appear on shows with Joan Rivers, Jay Leno, David Letterman, Merv Griffin, Neil Cavuto, and others. It was all great fun, and over the years, I think I got better at the give-and-take with these hosts. (You can see them at my website, *richardthalheimer.com*, and also on the YouTube channel, The Legend of Sharper Image.)

A movie or series placement for product or company exposure is also great if you can get it. The Sharper

Image got one of its first meaningful exposures in the James Bond movie, *A View to a Kill*, and later, in the Billy Crystal movie *When Harry Met Sally*. He and Meg Ryan did a great scene in a Sharper Image store in New York. This type of coverage is what you dream about in any business. We've also been mentioned many times on late-night talk shows, used in syndicated comic strips, and included in television sitcoms, like *Friends*, *Sex and the City*, and *Will & Grace*.

The filming of the *Sex and the City* episode was especially fun, because some Sharper Image executives, and

my wife Christina, and I, were invited to be on set. The star in this episode was the engaging Kim Cattrall. This particular episode took place in our store at 57th and Fifth Streets in New York City, our flagship New York City store, which always attracted many famous clientele. It was great fun watching the taping, and meeting Kim. She was really nice, and we thoroughly enjoyed the day. Of course, the episode of the show got us lots of attention, and it was free publicity as well.

BUZZ-GRABBING IDEAS

How can you get coverage for your business? Consider doing something charitable with a local organization. Maybe you could host an event. Or you might do something wacky or off the wall, or maybe promote an unusual contest or some sort of a newsworthy giveaway. Whatever you decide to do, of course, make sure the local media is aware of it.

Did you hear of a gas station selling gasoline at the 1990s prices for 90 minutes at 11:10 p.m. on the last day of the last century? Well, I didn't either, but if someone had done that, I suspect there would have been long lines to buy gas for 90 cents a gallon and a lot of reporters to cover it.

Certainly, at the time it happened, we all heard about Madonna kissing Britney Spears in the 2003 Music Video

Awards in New York City. That was a kiss heard round the world.

Then there was the infamous 2009 MTV Video Music Awards, when Kanye West interrupted Taylor Swift's award acceptance speech, grabbed her mike, and then shouted that Beyonce should have won the award for Best Female Video. I did not like his behavior, but these are the sort of publicity stunts that live for many years. Getting in the local or national press is great for your business. So, be creative. See what you can do to get there.

CHAPTER FOUR

HOW TO WORK WITH YOUR TEAM

One thought above all has guided me, and I encourage you to adopt it as well: Always speak and think of others as working *with* you, not *for* you. This makes a big difference in how you treat them and how they respond.

YOU'LL MEET THE SAME PEOPLE COMING DOWN THE LADDER AS YOU DID CLIMBING IT

You've heard that one before, along with "what goes around comes around." People have memories, and people at businesses have memories, and it's a lot better to leave a good memory. In everything you do, you create a reputation for yourself and your business. If you take advantage of someone, that person is likely to cause you problems later in your career.

Don't create a grudge for someone to carry. You don't want someone out there looking to get even for the way you treated them 10 years ago. To paraphrase a Chinese proverb, "Don't muddy the puddles along the road. You may need to drink from the same ones on your return trip." Build a reputation of fair and even-handed treatment of your colleagues and in your community. Doing so may be most important in the business network where headhunters and recruiters are always calling around for references, including the places that someone has worked in the past.

I believe in karma. Your good karma helps you throughout your career, and bad karma will hurt you eventually. Stay positive. There's no good reason to have enemies. You want all the support and all the positive word of mouth you can get. Even when people don't get along with me, I try to part ways with them on good terms.

At the Sharper Image, we always threw good-bye parties for people who were leaving, even to take another job. It may seem odd to provide a nice sendoff for someone who resigned, but sending a message of appreciation for years of service showed we wish them well in their next job and there are no hard feelings. That conveys to the remaining employees that we're a good place to work because we have such a positive outlook. It creates a better reputation for the company.

In fact, we often had the experience that former employees asked to work for us again, and I always encouraged the manager to accept their application. It too was good for our reputation.

What could be better word-of-mouth for The Sharper Image staff than to know that, after working somewhere else for a year or two, Joe in accounting wanted to come back to us? That is a wonderful endorsement of our company. We must be a better place to work than everyone thought because Joe checked it out and decided to come back a year later.

ASSUME MAKES AN ASS
OUT OF YOU AND ME

Think about it, the word assume, ASS-U-ME. "Assume makes an ass out of you and me" is a silly saying, but hold on, it's true. You've probably had this experience: You assigned a task, left a message, or made a request, then assumed it was taken care of. But the person didn't get the message or didn't follow through. Because you assumed, you didn't follow up in time. In real life, though, a lot of things just don't get done at all or at least not right away. To ensure your success in business, *never* assume.

On everything that is really important to you, follow up to make sure it gets done on your schedule and to your standards.

Following up isn't the same as doing the job yourself. Learn both to delegate tasks and to verify their completion. If you find out they're not done as you expected, don't get discouraged. Realize no one is perfect, and humans are not robots. They don't always get things done in the right order or on the quickest schedule. You might find they need more support or training. Regardless, humans are not robots.

Often in my business or personal life, I've had to follow up one, two, or three times before the other party responds. The delay isn't necessarily that they don't think that I'm important enough. Maybe they're busy, maybe they know I'll let them take care of something else first, maybe they just don't know how to prioritize their work, or maybe they feel they have nothing to report because they gave up too soon. At The Sharper Image, for example, I've often asked someone if they've reached the vendor about a product that I asked them to look at. As often as not, they tell me, "I left a message, but they haven't returned it," or "We're still trading phone calls."

When that happened, at least 75 percent of the time, we would pick up the phone, reach them, and get it resolved on the spot. Sometimes the vendor would say, "That's funny. I've been calling you and waiting for a call-back." Following up is so easy. I will venture to say most business success is not because of being brilliant but simply following up.

NO ONE IS IRREPLACEABLE, NOT EVEN YOUR TECH GUY

Computers and software programs can help us in so many ways, but they can also cause us grief and expense. Sometimes the people who manage them can be difficult. I'm thinking of one of our computer programmers from years ago. He was brilliant, the only one who really knew what was going on with our software systems, and he wasn't about to let us forget it. He was conceited, arrogant, and selfish—all of which made him difficult to work with. After about two years, we decided we had had enough of his tantrums, so we devised a strategy to build up enough bench strength to transition him out of the company. It was an arduous, time-consuming job, but what a relief when he left!

From that point on, I vowed that no one, regardless of how brilliant, was going to dominate our information technology (IT) area, and we kept that vow.

CUSTOM SOFTWARE, BIG MONEY,
AND DELAYED DEADLINES

IT can be a money sink and a challenge to decide where to allocate your resources. In general, I like to spend as little as possible, as slowly as possible. I don't want to purchase the latest program at the highest price because my experience has shown me it doesn't pay. It's just too fraught with expense and bugs. We built a lot of exclusive software, and we bought a lot of expensive software.

In the mid '80s, we were putting in a new order-processing system that we had worked on all summer. It was supposed to be ready in August, then in September, but by October—almost the Christmas selling season—it still wasn't working. The old software would not be capable of handling the crush of orders, so we faced a disaster. We were stuck in this gap between the old and the new.

An excellent computer consultant named Leo helped to get it all working but only at the last minute. How did we get so far behind schedule? That's often the way it is with new software projects. This experience taught me never to put critical software in place without building in many months to work out the bugs.

PEOPLE LIKE TO KNOW HOW THEY FIT INTO THE OVERALL BUSINESS PICTURE

I've already talked about the value of manners in dealing with your customers and suppliers. They're every bit as important when you interact with your staff. From fancy top-floor offices to warehouse packing floors, you can often observe bosses who forget that their employees have feelings. People don't like to be treated as anything more than cogs in a business machine. They want to be respected and treated as individuals.

Treat everyone with respect, courtesy, and profes-sionalism, and encourage those you work with to do the same. Then, when you're making a request, involve them in the reason for it. Explain why you're asking them to do a particular task. "Jerry, could you please pack this mail order first? If we can get it on the UPS trailer within the hour, the customer will receive it one day sooner than by the trailer that leaves in six hours."

That way, you'll accomplish tasks, train, and build better relationships at the same time. You'll also notice who's picking up on the training and the logic behind the requests, which will help you identify your future supervisors. There is always so much to learn about how to do a job better and how that job relates to other parts of the company. Each time you give someone direction, you can share your knowledge about how their job fits into the bigger picture, why some of their ideas are good, and others are perhaps not, and about your business in general.

UNDERSTANDING THE BIG PICTURE
AND THE SMALL DETAILS

The managers and the supervisors in your company should not only have a big-picture grasp of their own job, but they should also know the details of the positions held by the employees who report to them. If they don't, that's a big red flag.

Every manager won't know everything that everybody is doing. But if you repeatedly ask them for details about projects they're supervising, and they consistently don't know the details, they're not adequately detail-oriented. I've just seen it happen too many times.

Don't accept repeated responses like, "Oh, I don't know the answer, but I can find out and get back to you" without taking action.

People who can't balance the big and the small pictures don't know enough to manage well. I'm thinking of one executive who worked for me in the early years. Although he was competent in many respects, he didn't concern himself with the details of the department he supervised. We used to go back and forth about this: I would keep asking him to keep track of the details, and he would tell me I worried too much about them when I should be focusing on the big picture. I would reply, "Actually, if you would focus on the details, I could quit worrying about them and focus on the big picture." Of course, we didn't last much longer. He moved on to a company where he could leave the details to others.

THE BEST TEAM HAS DIVERSE, YET COMPLEMENTARY PLAYERS

Embrace different yet complementary types of people, mix personalities, and make sure they all get to know each other and respect each other. The best-working company often has the most diverse people. That was always true of The Sharper Image. Our ethnicities, backgrounds, geographical origins, and almost everything else varies widely. We laid our foundation on the principle of zero tolerance for sexism, racism, elitism, or any other ism.

We developed a culture that values respect for others, an even-handed approach to promotions and raises, and a contagious camaraderie. Throughout my time in the company, we held regular gatherings to communicate what's going on in the company and to give employees a chance to socialize with people at all levels.

Mixing a wide range of people with complementary skills turns out to be a sound approach to hiring and staffing. So does never tolerating backbiting or office politics. We also encouraged everyone to have a life outside of work, which might be one of the reasons they bring fresh energy and experience to their jobs.

PRAISE IN PUBLIC, CRITICIZE IN PRIVATE

Perhaps the best management advice ever written is, "Praise in public, criticize in private." Following it will give you better odds of being a successful and well-liked manager. I'll take the advice a step further: When you criticize, avoid emotion and personal attacks. Insulting the person's abilities will do nothing to guide their thoughts towards what they can learn from the situation.

Some very successful executives are known for their volatile tempers and their yelling and screaming; however, I don't see how that could ever be helpful. One prominent example of this is my friend Steve Jobs. He was known at Apple for his harsh criticism and sarcastic put-downs of subordinates, and he did it publicly. Steve was always polite to

me, but he certainly had trouble in his relationships with his employees.

Your objective should be to get a better result from the person across from you, not to hurt their feelings. So, if you make the conversation unpleasant, nasty, or personal, they will be thinking about the hurt instead of thinking about how they can learn from the situation. Keep the tone polite, calm, and objective. Focus on what you need to get accomplished and how they can help you achieve that goal. Talk about the specifics of work performance, job objectives, and techniques. Your purpose should be to get them on your side and move in the direction you want.

If the relationship looks as though it ultimately will not work out, you may need to issue a verbal warning, which may lead to future verbal and written warnings. Even then, keep a matter of fact, even-tempered tone.

A reputation for being even-tempered and positive goes a long way. Be free and public with your compliments. People love to be praised.

CHAPTER FIVE

THINGS CHANGE OVER TIME

When I first started, there was just me and one other person. As the orders increased, we added two more people to support us. As it happened, eventually one member of the staff wasn't working out, so I experienced my first instance of shuffling the staff so that we could continue to grow. Balancing workload and staff size was one of the most difficult things to learn.

MOVING SOMEONE OUT OF A JOB CAN BE A POSITIVE STEP FOR BOTH OF YOU

Not many people are good at delivering negative news to someone they supervise. Whether it's terminating a job, rejecting a vendor's product idea, or giving a verbal warning, do it in a way that sends them in the right direction with a more uplifted spirit. You'll both feel better, they'll like you better for it, and who knows, they might be back someday with a better idea or in a different capacity. Besides, it's good karma to spread positive energy.

Consider this example of what not to do, "Mike, I'm sorry, your work has not measured up. You've received three verbal warnings and three written notices. You just haven't cut it. I have no choice but to fire you. Good-bye, Mike."

Now let's try a much more positive and constructive approach. "Mike, I know you've tried your best. It's unfortunately still not meeting the minimum requirements for this position. This probably is not the right one for you. That's why I'm removing you from this position. Let's look on the bright side. You're an interesting and talented person. You're heading up from here, seriously, because tomorrow you'll think, 'Hey, I'm going to find a job I really enjoy and will excel and succeed at.' I'm confident you will. Good-bye, Mike."

Use your own language, but whatever you say, make sure you show respect and concern. It's appropriate to show you take this seriously. Anyone losing a job is naturally worried, so demonstrate your sincere belief that Mike is a good and capable human being, and he will excel when he finds the right job for him. If they're not good at or interested in their work, they aren't fulfilling themselves and won't prosper. By guiding them towards the potential for success, you can be sure you're helpful.

WHAT ARE PEOPLE REALLY WORKING FOR?

People may spend more time at work than they spend with their family. If you make their time at work as pleasant as possible, everyone will do a better job and get more done. So many intangibles go into satisfying work life. Your job is to discover the benefits that make work enjoyable and meaningful and provide them as much as possible. Those benefits are related to people's reasons for working.

People work for a lot of reasons. Money is a big reason, but as a manager, you need to realize that it's not the only one. A lot of people work because they love what they do. Or they work because they get recognition, which satisfies their ego. Sometimes the fringe benefit— a title or a nice office with a window view—goes a long way to satisfy some people.

For others, it's the opportunity to work from home one or more days a week, which technology as well as COVID-19 changes have made more accessible. It often doesn't matter where you work, so for those people with long commutes to the office, you may find out they would rather telework regularly and that they get more done by not spending an hour or more in transit.

Other motivating intangibles that can lead to tangible benefits include stock shares or stock options in the company. A lot of people enjoy the pride of ownership that comes with being a part-owner, even if it's only a small part. Work-life balance is also important to many people. For example, The Sharper Image always encouraged a healthy family life and a personal life that has time for exercise and outdoor activities.

And, if there's one thought above all others that has guided me and can help you, it is to encourage you to always remember to speak and think of others working *with* you, not *for* you. This is a big difference in attitude and respect. It makes a healthy relationship even better.

HOW AND WHY BUSINESSES CHANGE

Just like people, businesses change over time. The small business that I originally started was just one employee and me. A year or two later, there were three employees and me. A year after that, we were 10, and a few more years brought us to 25. By 2006, The Sharper Image had almost 4,000 associates, including executives, managers, sales associates, and distribution-center workers. As the business changes, the resources and skills it requires also change. For example, when we passed the $100 million mark in sales, we needed different skills than when we started. Passing $750 million in sales required still different skills.

When you start, you need people around you who get things done. They're the take-charge, type-A types. About 10 years later, you may find that those same people sometimes get in the way. Maybe they don't like working in a team, they have problems delegating or are incapable of learning to supervise others. To make it worse, perhaps they don't want to be supervised themselves.

So, be prepared, keep your eyes open, and manage the transition. Getting it done is still essential, only now an entire team—and not just one-star player—has to work together to do it. Same thing in sports: You need a team that likes each other, shares the glory of success, and avoids backbiting and office politics.

Resist the temptation to treat your business like your favorite pair of comfortable shoes. You might want to wear them forever, but eventually, you'll need a new pair. The life of every business is filled with transition periods, and sometimes they're painful. Change is true, evitable. The most successful entrepreneurs accept it and are ready to adapt to it.

YOU'LL DO EVEN BETTER WITH A
GREAT RIGHT-HAND PERSON

Through my business years, one fact that jumps out at me is that the business grew more easily whenever I had a terrific right-hand person helping me. Most people are stronger on either the creative or the administrative side. I like to think I can do both well, but I'm more productive when focusing on just one or the other. Suppose you decide to live on the creative side. In that case, you'll need someone to administer the daily details and vice versa: An operations person needs a specialist in creativity, marketing, and sales campaigns.

In the early 2000s, my right-hand person was the president and Chief Operating Officer, an incredible contributor that made the business grow more robust and faster than ever in our history.

Part of what worked so well about that collaboration was our compatible personalities. On the other hand, an inconsistent person will bring negative energy; you will only waste time arguing over who's doing what and who gets to make the decision.

It's worth your effort to find someone who compliments your skills. That way, you can make the best use of your time, and they can free you up by taking on the parts that you don't want to do or are less skilled at.

WHO'S REALLY RUNNING YOUR BUSINESS?

If you started the business, you probably assumed that you're the boss, which is a fair assumption. Then you hire a right-hand person, which should work out great as I mentioned in the section above. But it's not great if they start acting like they're the boss before you know it. If you stay in business long enough, it's likely to happen.

As the company gets bigger, it may also happen just within a department. Maybe the person hired to be the second in command in the merchandising department is attempting to take over its leadership. The vice president asks you to help reign in the person who's bucking for the VP's job. It can be healthy to let the friction evolve for a week or two if it shakes up a stagnant group. Eventually, though, you'll have to step in to control the chaos by making a tough decision.

Maybe you see this as your opportunity to push out a stagnant leader, but there are higher-quality approaches. You could give the ambitious number two a separate area to run. Or you might have to provide them with a choice: They can play with the team and support their coach, or they can leave, but continuing to create subversion is not an option. If you deliver this message fairly and honestly, they will usually receive it well. You may also be able to let them know that demonstrating consistent performance will eventually pay off in the form of a promotion.

A variation of this problem is when you want to bring in someone with more experience to supervise the department's former head. This doesn't often work out. Your best chance is to sit down with the former head, explain that the business has grown quite a bit, and it's time to bring in more talent. Tell them you hope they'll stay and work for the new person.

It's best if the change happens in the context of a department reorganization with an announcement and new titles for both the former and the new supervisors, along with a salary increase for the former one. That can transform what could be an ego blow into more of an ego buildup. Because people take a lot of pride in what they do, you don't want to create the impression that the former supervisor couldn't make it. Instead, announce that the company has grown and the department is being enlarged and reorganized. Then introduce the structural redesign.

MANAGE PEOPLE'S EXPECTATIONS — KEEP THEM ON TRACK FOR YOUR BUSINESS

As I've mentioned, people want to be respected, liked, and heard. Anyone who has run a successful small or medium business knows that one of the real keys to building a business is regularly communicating with your staff. That can include something as small as one-minute one-on-one chats about how someone's daughter is doing at school, or how they enjoyed their last vacation.

Short and personal (but not too personal) conversations keep you in touch with the human side of the people you work with. Check in with them every month or so. You could invite them to your office or drop into theirs and let them know how well things are going. Ask what they think about how things are going. I like to ask, "Hey, Mark, are you enjoying what you're doing? What do you like best about your job? What do you like least about your job? I'd like to hear that because I want to know what you're doing and how to make it better for you."

You might say, "Are you enjoying what you're doing? If you could delegate some part of your job, what would that be? I want to know how to make your job as enjoyable as possible."

Of course, we all have some tedious tasks (I certainly do.) But I start thinking about how to improve things for Mark only if he gives me some guidance on the things that need improving. Also, if Mark tells me he isn't enjoying the main part of his job—what I consider his highest priority, I know I should move him into a job he would like doing and replace him with somebody who would like doing Mark's current job.

I've also found it valuable to ask directly, "By the way, where do you want to be a year or two from now?" This gives you a more reliable picture of what they're thinking. If that's moving in a direction that works for your company, great; you can help them get there. But if their response suggests a disconnect between your goals and theirs, you know to start planning a replacement or remedying the situation.

While helping you connect with the people who support your business, keeping in touch also helps you plan it. You can use those communications to decide who's going to be doing this job in a year, who's going to be helping you, and where the business is going.

CHAPTER SIX

HOW TO NEGOTIATE A BETTER DEAL

So much of negotiation is learning how to respectfully find out where the rock bottom of the negotiation is without insulting the other side or sounding cheap. I don't pretend to be an expert on negotiating, but I will give you a simple and clear technique that has worked for me. It starts with the premise that you always want to compliment the other side, even when you're about to ask for a significant concession or a better price.

If instead you tear down their reputation or cause them to lose face, especially in front of other people, you make it difficult for the other side to give in. When people are insulted or shamed, they're in no mood to hand you what you want.

Keep things as positive as you can as you lead to your request. Tell them how much you value the relationship, how much you appreciate the product they supply, or what a great business the two of you have had in the past and can continue to have in the future.

Having laid a positive foundation, you're ready to take step two. Explain that despite how good the product is, or what an expensive process is required to produce a great quality product, the simple fact is this: "We will do a lot more business together, and our relationship will continue to be successful but only if we can get to the price point that works for both of us. How can we do that?" Again, clarify that the issue is *not* that their product isn't worth what they want to charge for it. Say you want to make it work, but if the product does not perform well at that price, you're not going to be able to sell as many, or whatever your best argument is.

Now you've accomplished two things. You've started the conversation on a positive note by building them up, not tearing them down. And two, you've explained it is necessary to get a better price or term concession—not because they're wrong in any way, but because you want to maximize the overall sales and unit volume for both of you, and change is necessary to get there.

Step three is the right way to begin to close this negotiation. To find the bottom line, you might say something like this: "Mr. Vendor, thanks for offering to lower the price by 5% and waive the shipping costs. That's a great concession, and it means a lot to me. It shows what an effort you're making. Is that it, or can you go a bit further to make this work? However, I still should ask, are there some other areas of flexibility on your part? It's not that you haven't already offered a lot, but I really want us to be successful together on this. The sweeter the deal is, the more we can promote the product."

If they say no, respectfully and politely approach from another direction with the same objective. You might say, "OK, I get the point. There's not a single penny more to reduce in the price. I got that, but can we work out some other meaningful areas to add to the contract's overall attractiveness? For example, can you provide us with some display units at no cost? Or what about returns? We've been paying all the costs. Can you pick that cost up? Would that help sweeten the deal?"

I'm careful not to sound as though I'm nagging the vendor. Use a polite tone as you approach the request from several directions because you want to find out how much there is to squeeze out. In other words, where is the bottom of this negotiation? I'm also careful not to squeeze that last drop out of the negotiation. Leave a little bit on the table.

NEGOTIATIONS SHOULD BE A
WIN/WIN FOR BOTH OF YOU

When you negotiate with a bank or a large vendor like IBM, get the best deal you can, and don't concern yourself with what they're getting. These businesses don't need any help from you. My advice is very different, though, when dealing with suppliers and vendors that are smaller than you are or are equal in size. In those cases, the best negotiation is one in which you get the best possible deal for yourself *without* getting the worst possible deal for the other party.

Many people think they must get the very best price, but that's not the case. Price is only part of the overall equation. Performance, quality, delivery, and the relationship's quality are at least equally important—everybody must win for anyone to win.

Smaller vendors, distributors, manufacturers, or service providers often will go overboard, even to the point of underpricing their goods. This is not necessarily a good thing for you because when they don't make the profit margin they need, it will eventually be reflected in what you get. They will have to make up for the shortfall somehow—maybe by putting your order last, cutting back on the quality control, or substituting slightly inferior goods or services.

There's an important psychological factor as well. As in any human relationship, both parties need to respect each other and want to do a good job. You make it hard for them to want to put out extra quality and effort for you when you squeeze them so hard.

On the other hand, when you push them to the lowest price, and, at the last minute, you voluntarily give back a little, the attitude changes. Now they think you're generous, reasonable, and the type of partner they want to do business with. You've earned their desire to give you their full attention and perform their best.

When we introduced our electric cruiser bike in 2003, my manufacturing vice president kept complaining that the factory was unresponsive, slow, and noncommittal about delivery dates. I learned the real issue: They were losing money on every unit. No wonder they were dragging their feet. We agreed to pay them about 10% more, and, all of a sudden, they were eager to please us.

WHAT'S THE RIGHT STARTING SALARY WHEN YOU'RE DOING THE HIRING?

You're also negotiating the price in the conversation you have with people you consider hiring. There's no mystery in determining the pay for entry-level positions. It's easy enough to check around. At the medium and higher levels, though, it gets trickier because there are so many variables.

Let's say you're hiring someone from the outside for a mid-level position. They have a salary history if they've worked before. Suppose it is sort of in line with your expectations. In that case, I ask, towards the end of the first or second interview, "So, Doug, with the understanding your salary would be reviewed again in 12 months, what do you think would be a fair starting salary for you in this position?" I clarify that I'm not asking for the person's fantasy number rather, "What do you think is reasonable for your skills in today's job market, given our economy and would make sense for our company?"

That approach puts Doug on the spot a little. If he gives me a ridiculously high number, it makes him look bad, and he probably would not give me a number that's too low. So, he might say he'd like to make, oh, $60,000. If that's acceptable, it's always best to be able to meet someone's expectations. Someone who gets what they ask for tends to come to work with a positive attitude rather than a chip on their shoulder.

On the other hand, if he has given me a number that is a bit higher than I want to offer, or if I want to test the waters a bit, I'll say, "Doug, that's in the ballpark, especially with your skills, and I'd really like to see you join us. However, some other candidates with similar or stronger experience are asking for a slightly lower salary. Would you consider starting at $50,000, and, that way, you could get started with us today? With your skills and drive, I expect you will do well, and, eventually, you will get where you want to be."

This lets me see what he's thinking, and if he declines to come aboard for less, I can always say, "You're asking for more than we wanted to budget for this position, but we really think highly of you. Is there any other compromise between us that would work for you?" If he still says no, I have the option to say, "Well, fine, let me think it over. I really appreciate you and would like you to work with us. I'll call you tomorrow."

There's nothing wrong with letting it sit overnight, and when you call tomorrow, you can ask him if he has considered a compromise. If not, you can tell him, "You know, that's fine. I'm pleased to meet your number, Doug, because I want you to feel really positive about joining us, and I look forward to you starting soon."

It's a sound approach that shows you Doug's bottom position without losing face or embarrassing yourself. At the same time, you've left your options open to meet his number if you want.

THE BEST TIME TO NEGOTIATE IS WHEN YOU DON'T CARE IF YOU GET IT

What about a one-time experience in which building a relationship doesn't matter? Working with a big vendor is not the only time to squeeze for your most advantageous deal. Buying a car, a house, some other type of building, or a computer is an example of nothing more than a cold-blooded "best deal" negotiation.

Here's how to get it right: Schedule the negotiation for when you don't need the deal so you don't feel any pressure. Maybe you're sort of thinking of leasing an office space, trying to get a loan, or making an offer on a car, but you're not desperate to do so.

Respond to every offer from the other side with this response: "I think we're making progress. Is there any further room for improvement? I'd like to sleep on it overnight and get back to you." Later in the conversation, wrap it up this way: "I appreciate how far you've come. That's a terrific deal. You know, though, it's still a bit higher than what I had in mind. Let me get back to you. Thanks so much for your time." Then just walk out.

One of two things is going to happen. The other side will stop you from leaving and offer you yet a sweeter deal, or you're going to leave. If you want, you can call them back in an hour or a day and let them know you've thought it over and decided to accept their offer. The absolute worst thing that can happen is that the other side withdraws or changes the offer. But again, you don't care whether you get it or not anyway.

So either you get a really attractive deal, or you don't make a deal. In the second case, the technique works only if you haven't involved your emotions. If, on the other hand, you've fallen in love with the deal, which often happens during house or car shopping, that's a different situation. Avoid becoming attached to the outcome—you will get some terrific deals, and you will enjoy the process.

NEGOTIATING PLOYS YOU SHOULDN'T FALL FOR

People will often try techniques on you that are designed to do nothing but close the deal for themselves. Here's what to say to avoid getting sucked in.

If you hear, "What price do you have in mind?" don't disclose your price (unless you really lowball it). Just say, "You know, I don't know what it's worth to me today." Do encourage them to disclose their price. If, instead, you throw out what seems like a reasonable price and the other side accepts it immediately, you'll wonder how much you left on the table.

You may hear the other technique, "If I can meet that price, can we close this deal today?" Don't say "yes" unless you are sure you want the deal and have gotten the rock-bottom price. Don't accept the pressure. Give yourself an out for a day. Tell them that even if both of you come to a deal today, you still need approval from your boss, bank, partner, or spouse.

You could also respond this way: "Ms. Vendor, you've made a really terrific offer. I appreciate it so much. However, I promised Vendor Number Two that I wouldn't make a final decision until I visit them one more time. I won't use your price against them because I believe in keeping your bid in confidence, but I still owe it to myself and my company to hear their best price as well. So let me get back to you as soon as I've had a chance to talk with them." That might get you a better price on the spot from Vendor Number One.

And when you've chosen a vendor and price, contact them to say, "Your bid is great, and I know this is the start of a productive business relationship. Before I accept the price and let the other vendors know they're about to lose out on this, let me ask one more time, just to make sure, is this really your best offer, or can you make it a little bit sweeter?"

Then stop talking, and let them respond. If they say, it's the rock-bottom price, politely reply, "I understand.

Thanks for giving it one more look. Let's shake hands and make a deal." If they come back and say, "Well, we can knock another 2% off if you pay us in 30 days," or whatever, it was well worth asking.

THE ONLY FOUR WAYS TO PRICE YOUR PRODUCT OR SERVICE

The best way to price something depends on the situation and the time.

You have four choices:

1. A gain-market-share approach means pricing something low enough, so that the consumer chooses to buy your product, which allows you to grab market share. This is how Lexus carved out a substantial niche in the luxury-car market. The company deliberately priced its introductory flagship car at about $35,000, which at that time was easily $10,000 less than comparable offerings from BMW or Mercedes. Even if they lost money, their priority was to get positive word of mouth as they became known, so they could raise prices in later years. The strategy worked for them.

Another well-known example of this is Amazon. When it was first getting started, it lost money every year as a strategy to gain more new customers. The stock never got very high in its early years. In 1998, the stock was around $89. However, by October 1, 2001, the stock price was down all the way to $5.91. Why? Because it reported continued losses, and investors didn't believe it would ever make any money. Some said it would probably fail and go out of business. Jeff Bezos, the founder and CEO, kept telling analysts that the long-term strategy was sound, and that he would keep investing money in gaining market share, even if it meant years of continued losses. Eventually, he was proved correct, and by August 2020, Amazon was over $3,300 per share!

2. The value/benefit relationship is a common-sense approach and comes down to these questions: What benefit does this product provide? And what will people pay for it? This approach combines your own experience, with some research: You could ask potential customers what they are willing to pay and also search Google or Amazon to see what other companies are pricing similar products, or, for a service, call some contractors. Your research will lead you to a price that reflects the value for that benefit.

Like the market-share approach, the value-benefit relationship doesn't consider the cost to manufacture the product or service. All that matters is what the customer wants to pay and what alternatives cost.

3. The "Ratio Relationship" involves applying a multiplier, or ratio, to the cost to manufacture or buy the product or provide the service. An example of a ratio is to simply double your wholesale cost. This approach ensures that what you pay for the product or service, and what you sell it for, allows the business to make a profit. This is referred to as the gross profit, that is the selling price minus your cost. When you figure that amount, remember that the customer doesn't know or care about your costs, so applying a multiplier to arrive at the retail price may not result in a good value/benefit relationship. You don't want either extreme: a crazy high price that no one wants to pay, or a too-low price that doesn't take advantage of the market's willingness to pay more.

4. Lastly is the "whatever the market will bear" pricing approach. This works best for a product with no competition, because it's the only one

of its kind, or rare, or essential in a shortage. You typically see this with rare collectibles like irreplaceable antiques or one-of-a-kind objects at an auction. You also see this with pharmaceutical drugs when the manufacturer has a monopoly on it. When the COVID-19 virus was spreading in March of 2020, you saw this with basic products like hand sanitizer. Some people were able to get two or three times the normal price, simply because there was so little inventory available. This is not what I would call the most ethical approach, but it can be a practical one, and people do it all the time. Have you ever bought 24 bottles of purified water at the supermarket for about 25 cents a bottle? Compare that to buying a bottle of water in a movie theatre, and you will see market pricing at work: that bottle will be over $2!

I use a blend of pricing approaches. I want a normal ratio of cost to retail. I want a good value/benefit relationship for the customer. I want to grow market share. Realistically, I want to approximate the price that the market will bear. Put all these thoughts together, and you will soon arrive at a price for your product or service.

CHAPTER SEVEN

MANAGING YOURSELF AND YOUR EMOTIONS

I n business, you hear a lot of advice, and you learn a lot by experimenting to see what works. Especially when starting out, you get a lot of conflicting advice. Eventually, as the years go by, you are more confident in your own decision making. That was certainly true for me. Let me share some of the advice and experience that helped me build a big business over decades.

DECISION MAKING AND RONALD REAGAN'S FAMOUS QUOTE

When former US President Ronald Reagan said, "I listen to everyone's opinion, and then I make up my mind," he might not have known it, but he was giving great advice to company leaders. Let's take one half of it at a time: When you listen to everyone's opinion, not only do you learn more than when you talk, but you also validate the person who is speaking. By asking for their opinion, you make them feel important. Go further by encouraging honest opinions, not just "yes" because you're the boss.

One of my favorite techniques is to present the problem to the group, maybe layout—without showing bias— varying arguments, and then ask each person to give their opinion. Ask everyone, regardless of their place in the hierarchy of the group. I tell them, "There's no right or wrong answer. I just want to hear some different opinions."

When you do, you may find that a consensus begins to emerge. That's when the second half of Reagan's comment kicks in: Having listened, the discussion may or may not influence your opinion. As the leader, you make up your own mind.

ACCOMPLISH THE IMPOSSIBLE
BY BELIEVING IN YOURSELF

It seems like, through my entire career, someone has always been there to tell me that this or that can't be done or if it can, it won't succeed. Stay strong. In the words of my favorite fortune cookie, "The most satisfying thing in life is doing that which others say you cannot do." It's true. Do you find that sometimes, or maybe all the time, others meet your ideas with skepticism? Or what if they tell you they don't think it can be done? Have you heard these kinds of reactions a lot? I certainly have.

It is extremely satisfying when others tell you that you can't do it, whatever it is. Satisfaction *is* sweeter when it is a result of overcoming odds. But, you might ask, why do you even have trusted friends, advisors, and professionals giving us their best advice if we're not going to listen to them? If you do listen, what do you do when your own best judgment tells you to forge ahead anyway?

Studies have repeatedly demonstrated that when confronted by a contrary opinion from the group, a decision-maker is likely to stick to their own opinion if just one other person agrees with it. But losing that ally makes the decision-maker more likely to adopt the group's opinion. For much of my life, my father has been my ally. During many depressing months or years when it seemed that nothing would succeed, having him to support my ideas made all the difference in the world.

Being the only one to believe in yourself can cause you pain and make you lose sleep. If you turn out to be right in the end, you're a genius. Think of Ted Turner starting CNN, back when nobody believed that a 24-hour news station could survive. Well, he was right, and he proved himself to be a genius.

But what about the worst-case scenario? You go ahead with your idea that everyone said wouldn't work, then it fails, and you lose a lot of money and reputation. That's a terrible result, but that's what being an entrepreneur is about—especially if you can learn from the failure and turn it around.

To help protect against disaster in the first place, don't risk everything you have on your next move unless you are incredibly confident about the outcome. Save something, so that if it doesn't work, you can try again. My first *Runner's World* watch ad was doing great, so I decided to take a chance on a much bigger magazine, *Popular Science*.

The ad was about $60,000, a huge jump over the $1,000 a month I was paying for the *Runner's World* ad. But I figured that even if I did just one-fifth as well, it would still break even. So I went ahead with the confidence that the odds were in my favor. That ad did well, too, so I decided to try a Sharper Image color catalog based on a strong hunch that since the magazine ads had performed for me, they would work in a catalog format.

As I mentioned in an earlier chapter, the catalog, which cost a lot more money than I had, would have bankrupted me if it hadn't performed. In risking everything, I ignored the advice I'm giving you but not the part about believing in yourself. Fortunately, that first mailing did well enough: I didn't make any money on it, but I didn't also lose any.

The obvious strategy was to figure out what products worked, when which sold the best, and which lists I mailed to did the best. All I had to do is follow the guidelines that are now laid out for me in black and white. What products did the customer tell me they liked? What groups or lists of people responded to my offerings? That's what I personally love about direct response and, in today's world, Internet advertising. It immediately gives you the data you need to form new conclusions to lead you into new and more productive directions.

My idea of putting the catalog online in 1995 when websites were becoming popular was met with more skepticism than you can imagine. A lot of people, including my own Board of Directors, trusted associates, and even some of my best advisors, told me it wouldn't work. Because I believe in myself, however, I knew it was worth a try. We did eventually launch the online store, and it became a substantial part of our business.

NO GAIN WITHOUT PAIN

One of my favorite clichés has been "no pain, no gain." I kept a paperweight inscribed with it on my desk, and for many years, I believed it, especially after The Sharper Image's painful transition that started in 1989. That was the year of the only financial loss in our history, and we had significant employee layoffs. We had to totally rethink our business strategy to begin manufacturing our own products.

Since that was such a painful period, I concluded that the slogan must be right. You cannot get gain without pain. I suppose my experience in various exercise programs taught me the same lesson. Some pain is unavoidable to get the eventual gain.

Then we had a number of good years, even some record years, and not much pain at all. In fact, we had a lot of fun. So I decided that the more likely truth is that success often follows many years of hard, painful work. I hid the paperweight in a drawer.

Let's use the analogy of sailing in the ocean. Sometimes, the wind is at your back and you're flying along, while at other times when you're tacking upwind, you have to work yourself to exhaustion.

Woody Allen had a humorous way of making sort of the same point when he said, "Ninety-nine percent of success in life is showing up."

For me, staying committed for 35 years was a life passion and a huge effort. Of course, I loved it, but I certainly had some difficult times. Not everyone would have stuck

it out. However, if you can make the commitment, I prom-
ise you'll see huge results. Businesses are sometimes built
quickly or even overnight, but more often they have a lot
more staying power and quality when they're built over
a long time. Some years, you'll work harder than ever for
little or no gain, but they are likely to bring you to years
of easy success.

Oh, you won't get back an equal amount of success
for every amount of hard work. In terms of Pavlovian
psychology, it's like you're pushing this lever repeatedly. Sometimes, it gets you that little pellet of food, but
you never quite know exactly when you will. All you do
know is that if you keep pushing the lever, eventually
food will fall out.

HOW TO HANDLE THE DOWN DAYS

As I mentioned before, most entrepreneurs tend to look
on the bright side. But even optimists experience down
days. Bad days used to really get me down. After a number of years, though, I developed the confidence to realize that the world would look brighter after a good night's
sleep. My entrepreneur's optimism would often return
the next day.

There is so much discouragement on the road to success that you too have to learn how to cope with it. When

a down day happens, as it inevitably will, accept the fact it was disappointing, and tell yourself that things will look different tomorrow.

Let's say it's three o'clock in the afternoon and one of your largest accounts has just canceled or your computer just fizzled and it's going to cost you a lot to replace, or your most valuable associate unexpectedly quits on you at the worst time. Instead of dwelling in despair, here's what to do: Lick your wounds, feel really sorry for yourself, have a good dinner and maybe a drink, and try to go to bed as early as possible. Keep telling yourself, "It will be better tomorrow." Don't let yourself dwell on it too much that night because getting depressed is not going to help the situation.

You'll probably also find that when you wake up the next morning, things will not only start to look better, but you may also see some solutions. After you get over the despair and disbelief about what happened, you can begin to think about dealing with the problem. So when disaster strikes, go home, relax, and get a good night's sleep. I guarantee you'll start seeing solutions and feeling better.

GOD IS IN THE DETAILS

In the context of this book, "God is in the details" means that the execution of details often makes the difference between businesses that succeed and the ones that don't. In product design, it can mean how instructions are written, buttons, and controls operate, or pieces are finished or fit together. In my field, we say retail is detail.

In a retail store, the details include the professionalism of the display, the graphics, the cleanliness of the store, and the courtesy of the staff. I also really like an organized and well-designed dress code, if it is appropriate. In a service business like a restaurant, details might apply to the consistency of the food service, the quality of the presentation, and the taste and freshness of the food.

Whatever the business or endeavor, a certain "obsessive-compulsive" attitude about details sends a powerful message to new customers. Does this business have a consistent point of view and execution, or does the inconsistency or sloppiness discourage the customer from engaging with it? It's often cheaper to do things right the first time because you don't have to repeat it to correct the errors.

In every enterprise, it seems that a million details must be executed correctly. The next time you're criticized for being overly particular and picky in your approach, take it as a compliment. Don't be embarrassed because you want things done a certain way and other people have little patience with your exactness.

Steve Jobs, Apple founder and CEO, was known for his obsession with details. He would challenge his designers to look at the design, again and again, to continue to simplify and improve the result. He pushed for a long time before he was satisfied.

For me, one of the most detailed and time-consuming efforts was the introduction of our retro electric cruiser bike from Sharper Image Design. When we introduced it, I was surprised to learn that it was not in most of the stores I visited. I knew it wouldn't sell if our customers couldn't see it, so I made sure they could.

The next time I made a tour of stores, the bike was in stock but it was never charged up (it had blue LED lights

that glowed when it was), and the key for turning on the bike was never handy, which meant a customer wouldn't be able to see how the bike worked.

I started a program to put the bike up on a rear stand, so the wheel could turn, and I made sure the bike was charged and had a key. A month later, I watched customers look at the bike but not twist the throttle to see the wheel turn. So, we added a tag on the handlebar that said, "Try me. Twist the throttle." Properly presenting the bike took attention to one detail after another.

Here's how important checking the details is to me: By the time we had opened the 100th store, it was taking a lot of time to visit each store in person. But I still needed to get to every store once a year and get to know the manager and the top salespeople, so we bought a corporate jet. That's often a controversial decision because some people do not appreciate its value. For us, though, the jet became a really cost-efficient and effective way to get around because it allowed us to visit stores in three cities and be home by dinner time. It was a time machine that continued to enable us to visit every store even when we grew to 180 of them.

A STYLISH COORDINATED APPROACH INSPIRES CONFIDENCE

I love to see businesses that are coordinated in graphic style, colors, logos, even perhaps a uniform dress code for your people who face the public. It conveys when, say, a house painting crew shows up in t-shirts whose design matches the one on their truck. Or when everyone who works in a fast-food place wears polo shirts, caps, or aprons that match the tablecloths or placemats. Starbucks and, in California, In-N-Out Burger are examples of companies with great coordinated presentations.

We coordinated everything at The Sharper Image. Most stores had a modern black and white interior design that appealed to men and women alike and that showed off the colorful Sharper Image box designs. The store sales associates in black slacks and black polo shirts coordinated with the design. The same black and white theme carried throughout the website, the paper catalogs, and the boxes.

Over the years, even the paper catalog was designed with this theme, and the boxes which we designed had a coordinated look that conveyed the message that there is a coordination of design in all that we do. That's what it's about. You want to look professional, and that means clean, neat, and coordinated. The upfront costs of a professional and coordinated look may be high, although you might be able to get it done on the cheap. You can order pre-designed looks in online and catalog supply houses, including *VistaPrint.com*. Once you get over the initial expense, it won't cost you much more to buy supplies that match than supplies that don't match, so you're better off doing it right. Coordinated style makes a great first impression, and that goes a long way towards getting a customer back for a second impression and a third.

CHAPTER EIGHT

BUILDING THE PRESENT AND THE FUTURE

Another fact is that businesses have ups and downs, and that can be one of the most stress-ful times in your life. You wonder if you will get through these difficult periods.

We have mentioned the saying that it is easy to man-age in good times, and the real test of your management ability comes when you have a down time. Here is some advice to help you cope with the challenges.

CONSISTENCY IS THE HOBGOBLIN OF LITTLE MINDS

The funny phrase in the title means that you have to be willing to change your mind. To me, there is nothing more important than staying flexible, being ready to alter your course as soon as you learn something that warrants it. Life is so challenging that if you're not prepared to literally turn on a dime, it's hard to keep up and eventually get ahead.

Most people don't like direction changes. If you made a decision that everyone started to support, they won't be happy when it alters. So it's not enough to change only your mind. You'll also have to help your staff get on board with the new path by explaining why it's a good idea. I let them know that *I never change my mind until I have new information.*

If *you* have new information that affects the situation, why *wouldn't* you use it to make the best decision possible? You're responsible for doing exactly that.

As you work on selling the changes to your organization, it helps a lot if you show everyone respect for their contributions. Acknowledge the incredible effort they have already put in, and apologize for asking them to shift directions. Having incorporated the best information into your strategy and smoothed over the ruffled feathers of anyone who has to redo their work, the whole group is now moving towards a better goal.

FAIL YOUR WAY TO SUCCESS

The most important thing you can do to move in a positive direction is to take action, and as soon as possible. Do *something*. There's always the risk you may make a mistake in choosing a particular path, and that's actually a good thing. The sooner you find out you're wrong, the better off you are because now you'll try something else.

An entrepreneur's life is nothing like a bureaucratic job where the goal is to keep it for as long as possible without letting any mistakes show up. By contrast, you may need to try several alternatives and make mistakes to find the right course as quickly as you can.

You will inevitably take paths that turn out to be dead ends. In fact, many of the things you try won't work. Don't let it discourage you. The only person who never fails is the one who's afraid to try, and therefore never does, but also never has the opportunity to succeed. You can't succeed unless you're willing to risk failing.

I'm a good example of the value of "failing your way to success" because during the first 20 years of The Sharper Image, I tried so many things that didn't work. They include a health catalog, a spa catalog, spa stores, a wine club, even a home collection catalog. But I never let those experiences stop me from trying, and neither should you.

PLAN FOR THE WORST-CASE SCENARIO

It's unlikely that the worst thing that could happen will ever happen. It rarely does. But mentally preparing for it anyway is a good planning tool. If worst fears should materialize, you won't be caught off guard, and if things turn out well, you haven't wasted the effort.

Think about how you'll recover, finance your next effort, and make up the lost sales, investment, or effort. You'll sleep better at night.

Near the paperweight preaching "no pain, no gain" on my desk, I used to keep another one engraved with "No Surprises"—my subtle yet clear message to everyone who came to meet with me. Surprises—like a budget item is way out of line, some delivery is hopelessly late, or the quality of a delivered product is poor—can interfere with the day-to-day management of any business. For us, they negatively affected sales planning, especially around critical selling times like the holidays.

When The Sharper Image was a publicly-traded NAS-DAQ company, I was not the only one who didn't like unpleasant surprises. They were the last thing any fund manager or shareholder wanted to hear.

In a small business, a surprise like the resignation of a key executive can feel earth-shattering.

Because startups and small businesses tend to have less financial resilience, any event with financial consequences can drastically affect the ability of the business to provide adequate cash flow, make payroll, pay the bills on time, and meet its other obligations.

In a bigger business, each surprise has a smaller impact on the overall business. That was definitely true for The Sharper Image as it expanded, so I was eventually able to take *that* paperweight off my desk. Realize that there will always be surprises. But look forward to when your business has a strong brand and enough financial staying power that your business will survive a major surprise. Until then, hope for no surprises, but anticipate and prepare for them.

In recent times, Boeing Aircraft endured a major surprise that was a huge detriment to the company. Two disastrous crashes resulted in many lives lost and the need to ground the 737 Max jet. No one could have foreseen that the world's biggest maker of commercial aircraft would release a plane with a fatal flaw in service. Another type of crisis occurred in February 2020 when the COVID-19 virus shut down many businesses for an extended period. That was an incredibly difficult time for some businesses to stay afloat.

That was also the once-in-a-lifetime investing opportunity for gutsy money managers, because as it turned out, between the bottom of that market on March 23, 2020, and just six months later, many public stocks doubled or tripled in price! You can read some of these stories at my investing websites, *TheSharperFund.com* and *SharperInvesting.com*.

Here are some lessons I learned during my own ups and downs. Let's start with the most typical problem, which is you have a lot of good years and are caught by surprise when things get rough.

MOMENTUM TAKES ON A LIFE OF ITS OWN

As soon as momentum, whether positive or negative, gets going in your business, it comes with its own head of steam. Our unbroken run of successes from 1977 to 1987 covered a multitude of small mistakes, and sales growth continued. When we ran into problems starting in 1989, the momentum turned negative, and it took time to turn it around.

This is similar to the cycles of the US economy. A strong expansion or a downward spiral gives the impression that it's never going to end.

How can we take advantage of it in our own business? Use the periods of expansion to increase advertising, spend money to acquire customers, do lots of prospecting, and maybe try some marketing that normally might feel wild and crazy for you. Conversely, when things are contracting, cut all those frivolous marketing efforts, tighten your belt, and do all you can to keep morale up.

When The Sharper Image was suffering through poor financial momentum and bad press stories in 1990, we put posters up all around the company with this message: "Perception Lags Reality." I constantly reassured our associates that things were going to get better, and, in fact, that process to get there was already in place even if the positive results didn't yet show up in sales and earnings.

We got through that difficult period and entered our best one. In your business, I'm sure you'll see the same. Don't let the down periods get you down. Instead, start working to turn that momentum positive.

HAVE CONFIDENCE, EVEN WHEN YOU'RE LOSING SLEEP AT NIGHT

During the times when the very viability and future of your business is uncertain, you might feel strongly tempted to jump ship.

Some of your close associates will stick with you because they love the company, respect you or genuinely believe in your leadership to turn things around. Others will stay because they don't have a better option; so as long as they're getting paid, simple inertia will keep them in place.

Other associates, especially those who have little stomach for uncertainty or who see themselves on a fast track to success, will start looking for greener pastures. It can be a serious blow to your business to lose a critical position at a time like this, and it adds stress when you're already suffering from worry and frayed nerves. It can be one of the most precarious moments in the life of your business, especially if one departure snowballs into an even greater exodus of talent.

What to do? As always but especially now, be transparent with your people. Disclose that it's a critical time and that you really need and want them to stay. Give them an incentive, like extra compensation paid in a year or two or stock option grants or end-of-year bonuses that are guaranteed only for people who stick around to collect them.

While you're being transparent, keep your psychology upbeat and positive. Never demonstrate a lack of confidence or self-doubt. In a scene in the movie *Funny Girl*, Nicky, a world-class gambler, shows that whether he's winning or losing, he must always appear confident and in control. That's good advice. Although you should always own up to business challenges and never try to come off as superhuman, the fact is that as a leader, you need to convey confidence.

A NEAR BRUSH WITH BANKRUPTCY, OR "WHAT HOURS SHOULD YOU WORK?"

This is a funny story to me at least, and hopefully to you. Clearly, when you're working for someone else, it is great to show up early at the office and leave late. It makes a great impression. If you have to be in a physical place, you have to be there. At an office, you have a slightly different situation and if it's your own little business, maybe it's even more unusual. For many years, I made it a point to be the first one at the office and the last to leave. I follow the old adage, the boss should be the first one to arrive, and the last one to go home.

About 15 years after starting The Sharper Image, we had this terribly difficult year in 1989-1990. It was the first year in our history we ever had a financial loss. We deserved it. We had started to become inefficient and wasteful because we were spoiled from the preceding 15 progressively successful years in a row. We had not prepared to cope with adversity or to develop discipline.

For us as a management team, however, the painful experience was constructive. I thought hard about how we had gotten where we were and what we were doing wrong. As it turned out, we survived and became a stronger company. We learned to cope with adversity, and we became much better managers. Along with the layoffs I mentioned before—the first in our history—we created a new strategy for our merchandising. If we had not had to learn new disciplines, we would never have seen our best years of revenues and earnings after that.

During the worst of that time, one of our board members said something that really inspired me to work through our problems: "Richard, getting to this point took really good merchandising, which is pretty easy for you. Now you're going to prove that you can learn to be a good business manager as well."

Part of that process to become a better manager got me thinking about what was most likely to make us survive and how I wanted to spend my time every day. I had to rethink both my practices and my long-held beliefs.

One of those beliefs was that the boss should be the first to arrive and the last to go home as I did for 15 years. At some point during our financial crisis, I imagined The Sharper Image in bankruptcy court (we were never there) and my standing before the judge to plead, "Your Honor, be lenient with me because, you see, I showed up early every single day." Thinking about how silly that would sound brought me to this conclusion: I needed to do what's best for my business even if what's best is not to come into the office every day at eight o'clock. I realized that sometimes I do my best thinking by taking a walk in the morning or daydreaming at home on my computer or talking to people on the telephone.

Now, I come in only as often as necessary without feeling guilty, but it took me a long time to get there. (At least I didn't have to tell it to the judge!) Many days I work at home in the morning, maybe writing and answering emails, or I head into the office at 10 a.m. It makes a huge difference that I have a fantastic right-hand person and an accomplished management team to run the day-to-day operation and supervise all different aspects of our business, and our entire management team is really solid and accomplished. Obviously, that makes a huge difference. It's taken me a long time to get comfortable with this approach. It works for me, and thank goodness I didn't have to tell that to a judge in bankruptcy court.

HOW TO RESOLVE LEGAL DISPUTES FASTER AND LESS EXPENSIVELY

The years have brought many legal disputes between The Sharper Image and other parties. Some of the times our attorney's initial communication triggered a series of interactions that culminated years later in a settlement that cost both parties time and money. Because attorneys bill by the hour, they tend to let things drag on.

But some of these situations were business problems as much as legal, so if I had just picked up the phone and gotten personally involved, I could have solved a problem right away with minimal expense and aggravation.

For example, at the time of the 1994 earthquake in southern California, The Sharper Image store in Sherman Oaks was badly damaged. Our attorney at the time said we would be legally correct in closing the store, walking away from the lease, owing nothing. He was sure that the lease had a clause that permitted it. Our CEO at the time was working with our attorney.

When the case eventually went to trial before a judge, we lost and had to pay attorney's fees and damages of more than half a million dollars. Several years later, I happened to meet the nice owner of this building; he told me if I had just called him personally when this incident occurred, we probably could have settled the entire matter on our own without any attorney involvement for less than $100,000. That expensive lesson goes like this: When you have an opportunity to call up the opposing business owner and talk business—not law—you might reach a settlement and avoid legal expenses that benefit the attorneys, not you. I'll never make that big mistake again. I hope you don't make it the first time. Don't be afraid to pick up the phone and try to solve a business dispute disguised as a legal one.

PAY BILLS ON TIME—
THE CHECK'S IN THE MAIL

Like people, businesses develop reputations. One of the most important and long-lasting reputations your business will ever have is your credit history—specifically, how you pay your bills. Some businesses, especially the larger ones, take advantage of their smaller vendors by paying their bills late. If someone provides a product or service with the terms on credit and the due date specified, there is no ethical or legal reason not to pay on time. It's cheating, which becomes stealing if you don't pay at all.

Beyond the legal considerations, you are setting yourself up to get poor treatment from that vendor. Why would they want to give you their top-of-mind attention when you're their worst-paying account? I'd rather be their best-paying account, knowing they will give me great attention and follow-through. Plus, if you ever need to ask them for something like extended terms to get through a really lean period, they'll be more receptive if you've always paid them on time.

Even better for everyone, pay early and you'll probably get an additional discount. It's common to ask and receive about a 2% discount when you pay in 10-20 days.

When I started my office supply business, I'd type "Net 30 Days" on the invoices. I actually expected the check to arrive by the 31st day. When it didn't, I was so surprised. I would call them and ask, "Gee whiz, what happened?" My naiveté and my candor must have caught them off guard because then they actually would pay me. I learned you've got to personally follow up and nag these people. The businesses with the most money are sometimes the worst offenders, but you just have to be polite.

I've always made it a point to pay bills on time or sooner. People appreciate it so much, and they remember it if you ever need a favor.

CHAPTER NINE

BUSINESS OUTSIDE THE BOX

There is also a human/emotional side of business, which is what you learn by visiting with others, how you juggle your family with your business commitments, and how you handle your own emotions when you're not certain what to do or how to proceed. Here are some thoughts.

TURN YOUR VACATIONS INTO FOCUS GROUPS

Vacations are some of the best thinking times for entrepreneurs. You will see your business better when you're a little bit further away from it. I've also received some really good ideas from other people while on vacation.

When The Sharper Image was more of a men's store, I used to go to a spa resort that attracted a fairly high percentage of female guests. When I asked them what they thought about my stores, I heard consistently that they were unappealing—too technical, too cold, and too gray.

That feedback inspired a new store architecture that also appealed to women and resulted in a clientele that was equally divided in terms of gender.

How many people do you need to ask before you can count on the validity of their opinions? Are focus groups of just two, three, five, 10 people statistically reliable? My experience is that if I ask about 10 people the same question, a reasonably clear trend will emerge by the tenth answer. That isn't very many people, yet the number works as a valuable predictor.

Try it with one of your questions at work, maybe a problem you can't quite resolve. The 10 people you choose could engage with your business or they could be friends or strangers. You'll also learn something about whether the answers are similar or even split. I didn't use formal focus groups when I was CEO because it was easy to just ask people their opinion and listen to them. We saved a lot of money on focus groups and got great information.

Customers in particular are a ready source of tips on improving your business. I spent so many hours in the stores talking to customers and asking things like, "Tell me something you like about our business and something you don't like about it."

TRY A MINI-VACATION THIS MORNING

To avoid getting into a rut, I love to vary each week's routine. I might take off in the morning, or an afternoon and, occasionally, even the whole day. Well, I don't really take it off—I'm communicating at home or on the road to get some work done. Sometimes I work at home via phone and email, sometimes I drive somewhere and make cell phone calls on the way or something like that, so some work is definitely getting done. But by staying out of the office you get a sort of refreshing mini-vacation.

Mini-vacations can be essential for avoiding burnout if you're a business owner because you may not be easily able to take real vacations. Burnout won't help your business grow.

Remember that the growth of your business is like a marathon, not a sprint. You may have to sprint at times, but in general, it's better to pace yourself so you can stay relaxed. You have probably noticed that when your stress level is even a little too high, it can limit your productivity. Mini-vacations will help you keep your workload slightly below the stress level and keep you energized. As your business grows, avoid letting your stress grow at the same pace.

WORK, CAREER, MARRIAGE, AND FAMILY

Many marriages break up over one spouse's dedication to working—or maybe *over*-dedication to work. You probably know people who got divorced because one partner was too preoccupied with business. The mini-vacation will help to avoid this, too. Take time now and then to do things together, maybe a lunch or breakfast out or an afternoon spa trip for his-and-her massages. To show your spouse that they're on your mind, also remember and celebrate anniversaries, birthdays, and other important dates.

Let's add family and children to this mix. I am a complete believer in the value of family. I really believe in sitting down with my family for meals, going to my children's performances and sporting events whenever possible, and doing all the wonderful things that make family life great.

When it comes to a choice between spending time on family relationships versus building your career and staying late at the office, I chose the family first. You may be different. Have you heard the old one about the person on his deathbed reflecting on his life? He says, "Oh,

I wish I had spent more time at the office." (If you don't know that's a joke, you need to spend more time with your family!)

The moral of the story is that we are only here for a limited time, and there are a lot of valuable things to do. Work is one of them, but don't spend so much time working that you neglect time with your family and yourself because not doing so is actually most people's regret when they look back on their lives.

THERE'S MORE THAN ONE WAY
TO GET TO YOUR GOAL

Avoid getting frustrated by fixating on just one way to get where you're trying to go. If it's not working, try another way. The Sharper Image Design group and product-engineering group occasionally got stuck on something like a mechanical problem, and before long, that one stumbling block stalled the entire project. We moved forward by brainstorming creative approaches to accomplish the same objective.

Never believe that the path you started on is the only one that will lead to the finish line. But once you give someone the mission of solving a problem and start them in a particular direction, they will probably need your permission to take a radically different approach.

An alternative to trying something new is to drop the issue entirely. Let's say it's a feature you're trying to add to the product. Maybe the right solution is to just drop the feature, and not to combine it. This situation came up many times, when I realized I wasn't getting what I wanted, and the project was stalled for a few weeks or months.

One example was our Sharper Image Design best-selling eyeglasses cleaning machine. It was a great product, but we spent about five years trying to solve one maddening problem. This was for an eyeglass cleaner that you put your eyeglasses into, and it automatically cleans the eyeglasses, but here's the problem. After the machine cleans the eyeglasses, how do we get the liquid solution and the spots off the lenses?

This is similar to a typical dishwasher problem: When drinking glasses are cleaned, you don't want any spots on them. But at least in the dishwasher, there's tremendous heat. Our product, on the other hand, was battery-operated, so it didn't heat up, and spots remained.

It took me a few years to try a different approach: a secret silicone additive to the cleaning solution, which had the added benefit that the silicone material actually fills in microscopic scratches in the lenses.

Now when the eyeglasses are cleaned, and the cycle is finished, and the machine opens up and presents the eyeglasses, the customer removes them, and quickly and easily polishes the lenses with a microfiber cloth that customers can use at the end of the cycle to polish off the spots. Although we were asking them to go to extra effort, we turned that slight negative into a positive, by what we included in the washing cycle: a silicone additive that fills in microscopic scratches and improves the quality of the lenses.

The technique of creative thinking improves with practice. Step back from the problem, ask for a fresh approach, give your staff permission to try something different, and eventually, you'll find a new path.

MANAGEMENT BY OPPORTUNITY

If one guiding principle describes my recommended management style, it is management by opportunity. Business, like life, is always changing. Opportunities arise and disappear, obstacles pop up, then other ones do, and new solutions become apparent. It's the entrepreneur's job to think creatively, stay flexible, keep looking for the next opportunity, and do all you can to make it work.

As I mentioned in the previous chapter, not all the ideas I tried for The Sharper Image worked out. There was a Sharper Image Health catalog, there was a Sharper Image Spa catalog, there were Sharper Image Spa stores. There was a Sharper Image Wine Club, even a Sharper Image Home Collection Catalog that sold furniture and accessories. None of these concepts really succeeded. But the craziest idea I ever had, the one most likely not only to fail but to *bring down the whole company* was to manufacture our own proprietary products. It had remote odds of succeeding, but that ambitious idea was the main reason that The Sharper Image survived and prospered.

MY BREAKTHROUGH
PARTNERSHIP WITH STEVE JOBS

The potential for a breakthrough might be in front of you at this moment; the key is to recognize them when you see them. Early in 1996, I went to WebMania where I watched NeXT Computer founder Steve Jobs present his company's dynamic web page builder. At the time I thought, "I gotta have this."

Well, two months after WebMania, The Sharper Image launched its online catalog, which was built in partnership with NeXT Computers.

Later in the year, Steve Jobs visited my San Francisco store to hold a joint press conference with me. We announced that the new Sharper Image online store was powered by NeXT Computer's WebObjects platform. Why would you wait for a paper catalog to come to your

mailbox, when you could go online and see an entire store of products updated daily?

By then, John Scully had pushed Steve out of Apple, and Steve was really struggling with NeXT. To save the company, he had decided to go into the software business. We were one of his first major customers, and he wanted to get all the positive coverage he could.

Steve presented The Sharper Image website to a select group of press people and executives in our Sutter Street store in San Francisco, explaining that thousands of customized web pages could be built depending on information stored in a database.

NeXT Computer was using dynamic web pages with other clients, but this was the first time it was used on this scale within retail. As Steve said to our staff that day, "We will continue to enhance it, but it's already way ahead of anything else that is out there."

That year, Steve presented the software at a number of expos, using The Sharper Image's website as an example. In some venues, I also presented a short segment on how the website had allowed the company to transition from a traditional to an online catalog model.

At Internet World expo in 1996, I presented a segment during Steve's speech about dynamic web pages. The Sharper Image had spent $35 million to distribute two million paper catalogs each month to its clients the year before. This web catalog would completely transform how we do business.

The press referenced the partnership that Steve and I established as modern-day eCommerce. At the time, magazines such as Wired spoke about how the technology used by The Sharper Image and Steve's innovations were likely to change the retail sector forever. In the coming years, the model we worked on was offered and reproduced at other large retailers across the United States.

Digital content is now everywhere, with many effects, including the distribution of magazines and newspapers.

Many of the magazines we grew up with are no longer in print, and those that are, have gotten quite a bit thinner. In terms of news, I read more now than ever, but online, not on paper. Steve Jobs' breakthrough was to have a lasting influence, and I'm proud to have been there at the beginning.

It goes to show you never know for sure. Sometimes in life, a wave comes along, and you hope you have the instincts and the judgment to know when to get up on that wave and ride it. Some people might call it luck. I prefer to think that luck is really "preparation meeting opportunity."

If you have done your homework, you'll be able to climb the wave when it presents itself. When you ride it all the way in, others will say, "Wow, weren't you lucky!" But you'll know the truth: "Actually, I was prepared and took advantage of the opportunity."

GOOD THINGS COME TO THOSE WHO WAIT

A long time ago, I met Arthur Jones, the inventor of Nautilus Gym Equipment. You've probably seen or used their machines at some time in a gym that you've visited. The Sharper Image is known for introducing the first Nautilus machines available to the consumer for home use.

Arthur called me—I didn't know the man at the time—and said how much he thought we were the best place to launch his new line of smaller home machines, especially the first Nautilus abdominal machine, designed to trim your waist.

Arthur invited me to visit him at his Florida home, "Jumbolair," which had his private zoo and a 10,000-foot landing strip for his two jets, a Boeing 707 and a Cessna Citation. He used the 707 to bring elephants, alligators, monkeys, and other wild animals from Africa to populate his zoo at Jumbolair, and his original business was selling wild animals to zoos. (I don't approve of capturing and selling wild animals, but that was Arthur's choice.)

As a side note, eventually, Arthur's home and landing strip became the home for John Travolta and Kelly Preston. John is also an avid pilot who owned a 707 jet.

At his invitation, I flew to Miami. He planned to pick me up in his Citation Jet. I am at the designated pick-up spot, a private FBO. The jet lands and taxis in to meet me. A very nice-looking man strides out of the jet and toward me at the building. He is followed by a short scruffy guy that I thought might be the maintenance person. I say hello to the handsome guy. He says, "No, I am the pilot. That is Arthur over there." Pointing to the scruffy guy. That was typical Arthur. Very rich and very successful but very down to earth. We then got into his jet and flew the short hop to Jumbolair to visit and negotiate at his home.

Arthur's invention of the Nautilus machines was brilliant. He realized that people would buy a reasonably priced machine for their home, especially if it was designed to reduce the bulge in the stomach. I recognized its value immediately as well. When we featured the abdominal machine on the cover of our catalog, we sold thousands of them, more than we could have imagined. (What probably helped was the model, former Miss

Florida Terry Jones, Arthur's fourth wife. She was athletic and beautiful, and very photogenic.)

While we were working together, Arthur said one thing that stays with me even today: *Most people create something and make the mistake of cashing out too quickly. They don't realize they can maximize their results by holding out for the long-term.*

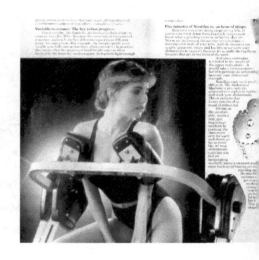

So when you're building your business or your career with a company, stick around long enough to see your results bear fruit. I worked and waited 30 years to see the tremendous accomplishments of The Sharper Image. Eventually, you'll be rewarded.

GOOD THINGS COME TO THOSE WHO ARE IMPATIENT

Stick it out, but don't dawdle in getting started. I'm always in a hurry to take the first step. As I mentioned before, you won't accomplish anything if you wait until all objections are overcome. That idea goes along with this one: The more impatient you are, the sooner you are going to get what you want. However, always be polite, of course. There's a delicate balance between being politely impatient and being rude.

Of course, patience is a virtue, and it also plays an important role in your business and personal lives. But certainly don't be reluctant to be impatient now and then.

When I first moved to San Francisco and started my office supply business, I would come down to the Financial District, knocking on doors, and walking the sidewalks of San Francisco, and I always kept thinking to myself, "People, get out of my way. I'm in a hurry, literally, to walk down the street to my next appointment. I'm in a hurry to get somewhere."

In Sharper Image planning meetings, my impatience translated to a sense of urgency to mail out five times the number of catalogs after seeing great results on a limited scale. While everybody else in the sales meeting was asking, "Shouldn't we go more slowly?" I responded, "Why? Let's get going!"

Once you see a course of action laid out before you, that's just the way I am. That sense of urgency to get moving and get something done is so important. Today, Elon Musk at Tesla is a perfect example of impatience resulting in a huge success. Elon is always pushing, and he sets seemingly impossible goals for his teams. He usually sets ambitious goals, which are not likely to be reached, and then he motivates them to stretch to meet them. His impatience has accomplished an enormous amount in a relatively short time. I admire him so much, and Tesla has been a great stock investment as well.

TOMORROW IS THE BEGINNING

You've got the ambition and the desire to make your business or your career more successful. It's not that hard if you're persistent. It bears repeating: You've got to take that first step, then think, *"Where do I want to be in five years or ten years, what steps are going to take me there, and how can I break them into small steps to actually get something done?"*

Once you do that first small step, you'll feel so good about yourself, and you'll feel ready for step two. Move forward every day, and before you know it, a year will have gone by, and you'll have accomplished a lot more than you ever imagined, and you'll be on the road to really building something even when you have to take a step back before you can take two steps forward.

Along with the many discouraging moments, you'll experience many moments of elation. It's great to be an entrepreneur and do your own thing. So have confidence in yourself, and I know you're going to get a terrific result. I wish you every success.

CHAPTER TEN

CHANGE IS CONSTANT

WHAT HAPPENED TO THE SHARPER IMAGE?

S o many years after the fact, some people still wonder, "What happened to the stores?" "How did the catalog make a comeback?" And even, "What happened to *you?*" Sometimes I am also asked, "Why is The Sharper Image brand appearing on products in large warehouse stores, and why is the quality of the product so different now?"

To answer those and other questions, let me walk you through my experience after my first book was released in 2004 through my departure, as well as some of what happened after I left. This chapter is the first full account of the journey; I never gave it all to the press.

In the first quarter of 2005, things, in general, were moving in the right direction. Our business was picking up, comparative store sales were improving, and our energy as a company with more than 4,000 employees continued to rise.

EQUITY FUND PURCHASES 12% OF COMPANY

In April 2005, I was surprised to learn that an outside equity fund from New York City, Knightspoint Partners, announced they had bought 12 percent of The Sharper Image's public stock in open-market purchases. They communicated to me their preference for representation on the Board of Directors as opposed to a time-consuming proxy fight. They also made it clear that if they were not given a place on the board in recognition of being the second-largest shareholder (I still owned 21 percent at that time), they *would* initiate a proxy contest to win the seats. This was not a friendly move, but I didn't want a proxy fight and I was open to fresh thinking.

FIRST VISIT TO SAN FRANCISCO, THREE BOARD MEMBERS RETIRE

I asked the two partners representing Knightspoint to come to my office, and we spent a couple of days together.

I liked them, and their ideas for improving profitability and stock price made it seem as though they genuinely wanted to help The Sharper Image. I thought that their experience could be of benefit to our board and our company. I also thought, "They have deep pockets and other access to capital that might be useful in taking the company in a new direction." Given the change in our markets due to the growing importance of the Internet, more capital was a priority.

Most importantly, I didn't feel that my position was threatened. After all, I was the major shareholder of the company, CEO, chairman of the board (with the majority of the board members being my own handpicked representatives). Beyond that, I was the founder and public face of the company, and lead creator of our best-selling Sharper Image Design products. And since we all wanted the stock price to go up, it appeared this could only be a win-win situation.

By June of the same year, I invited them to be on our board, freeing up the seats by asking three of our directors to retire. I left one seat vacant. In doing so, I avoided an expensive and distractive proxy fight, and all seemed well.

THREE NEW SHAREHOLDERS ON
THE NINE-SEAT BOARD

As time went by, I realized that this new arrangement was not working out as I had hoped. Frictions were developing. Our executives did not mesh well with the new directors, who were being too pushy and getting too involved in management duties.

In June of the following year, the board came together to appoint the third board seat to Jerry Levin, who had built a reputation as CEO at Sunbeam Corporation and Revlon. It wasn't until later that I would learn about his ambitions to push me out of the picture so he could become CEO. Though I did not see it at the time, it was evidently the case that he and the other new board members were actively plotting to oust me and remodel the company in their own image.

The story goes that Jerry, in a dramatic coup d'état, solicited board votes behind my back, and eventually persuaded a majority of the board to persuade me to resign. It hurt personally because I had been friends with my hand-picked board members for more than 20 years.

RESIGN OR BE FIRED

On September 12, 2006, I received a formal letter from the board, stating, "If you don't resign immediately, the board will fire you." My reply was immediate: "Fire me." I was *not* resigning from the company I founded.

Given my contract with the company, firing included significant compensation ($6 million), so I was also not going to resign and pass up the bonus. Jerry Levin was eager to become CEO, and he persuaded the board to pay me so he could clear the path for him to become CEO. I was fired a week later.

The very next day after the firing, I traveled to the Consumer Electronics Show in Las Vegas. I remember flying my little Cessna 182 to Las Vegas that day, and feeling so free—relieved of all my commitments and given back all my free time.

The firing was unexpected, but it certainly came with upsides. I was in a new marriage, with a one-year-old baby, and in some ways, I felt ready to reduce my time-consuming involvement in the business. I welcomed the opportunity to spend more time on my family, my hobbies, and my personal investing. I was still on the company's Board of Directors and the largest shareholder. And there was the $6 million payment that I received. So all in all, it wasn't a terrible fate. I was able to exit conveniently and cleanly, and get my time back.

But the experience was distressing. I was losing the business I founded, along with my work family.

Still, I recognized that the world was changing. By 2006, Apple was putting stores in every mall, competing with Sharper Image for "gadget" dollar spending; and the Internet had already significantly transformed the retail landscape, with Amazon becoming a powerhouse.

On the home front, my wife and many friends and other family members were concerned that I would become depressed and angry. Although I did feel hurt, my greater sense of relief surprised them. I would not have chosen this outcome, but, being the optimist I am, I looked on the bright side. I had so many things I wanted to do with my time, and the additional money in the bank was a bonus.

Time is such a precious commodity. I was elated to be done with my two hours of daily commuting. What's more, I had been working hard since I was 23 years old, and I was proud of how far The Sharper Image had come since 1977.

I still owned substantial Sharper Image stock, which gave me a remaining stake in wanting the company to succeed. However, I didn't have high confidence that the company would survive and prosper under Jerry Levin's leadership.

I realized that I wasn't the first founder and CEO to be pushed out of the company they founded. The most well-known example in recent times was when Steve

Jobs was replaced by John Scully, the former CEO of Pepsi Cola who had no computer business experience, so Apple went steadily downhill. Was that going to happen to Sharper Image?

DISTRESSING CHANGE IN STRATEGY

After I was removed as CEO, I attended two more board meetings and witnessed strategic decisions that I told the board would not succeed. From my 30 years of leading The Sharper Image, I had seen it all before. I knew what would work and what wouldn't. They showed they didn't understand The Sharper Image Design team's profit margins.

But it was evident that they were not interested in my opinion, and I had little power to affect change. Specifically, there was a lack of understanding of the profit margins made by The Sharper Image Design team. As the new guard embarked on their misguided strategy, I could only watch in disbelief. Though I was still officially a member of the Board of Directors, it was evident that I had little power to affect change. Things were continuing to get more challenging, and decisions were moving further from the cornerstones that The Sharper Image was built upon. That's when it became clear that they also wanted to remove me from the board. As part of that negotiation, they offered to buy my 21 percent stake in the company.

THE $27 MILLION DEAL

By May 2007, after six months of back-and-forth negotiations, we agreed to a price for my remaining shares of $27 million, about $9.25 a share. I was happy to get this money out, because I thought the stock would likely decline based on the new leadership I had witnessed. Anyway, it would have been difficult to sell such a large block on the public market, and cashing in at this time allowed me to make a clean break emotionally and financially.

On the day I received the payout, the news was released to the news media, and the stock jumped to $13 a share. The financial news and market bought into the spin that Jerry Levin would take Sharper Image to new heights of success!

DONALD TRUMP ON THE CATALOG COVER

In 2007, NBC's Celebrity Apprentice and Donald Trump were household names. The Sharper Image (after I left) launched its "new image" by promoting Trump Steaks on its June catalog cover. This first catalog cover by the new

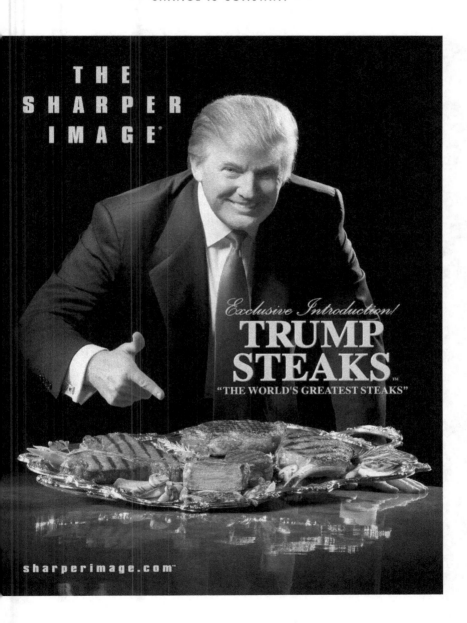

team was an incredibly poor marketing campaign. It was for Father's Day, The Sharper Image's biggest retail holiday of the year outside of Christmas, and the offer was a steak package for $1,000, an unusually high price point for the catalog.

Even more perplexing to me, the steaks were not available for purchase in our retail stores, which is odd for a Father's Day catalog, which should be promoting Father's Day gift sales. Not only did this unique partnership *not* sizzle, but it actually fizzled out after only two months. I knew I was seeing the beginning of the end, and I knew it had been a smart decision to "cash-out," and I felt good about the decision to sell all my stock.

SHARPER IMAGE STOCK FALLS TO ZERO

The final and complete payout to me arrived in late May 2007, and now I was completely out of The Sharper Image. Hard to believe!

The Levin team continued implementing their ill-conceived strategy. Not long after, on April 9, 2007, Steven A. Lightman became the president and CEO. The team expected that by December 2007, their new approach would produce positive results, and the all-important fourth quarter would show a robust sales and earnings result. An employee mentioned to me that the team bragged that the stock would double by that Christmas. Instead, the opposite happened. The 2007 holiday sales season was a flop, so the stock price dropped to a then-record low of 29 cents a share.

As a result of this strategic failure, the company was running out of money. Within two months, The Sharper Image stock went to zero, and on February 19, 2008, the company declared bankruptcy in Wilmington, Delaware. This was unbelievable, and it deeply saddened me that my namesake was declaring bankruptcy. Six days later, The Sharper Image announced it had received notification that it would be delisted from the NASDAQ exchange. As part of the bankruptcy process, which lasted over six months, the company closed 187 retail stores in 38 states, and 4,000 people lost their jobs.

POST-BANKRUPTCY, BRANDING AND LICENSING RIGHTS SOLD

On May 29, 2008, a joint venture led by units of four private investment firms—Hilco Consumer Capital, Infinity Lifestyle Brands, Gordon Brothers Group, and BlueStar Alliance won a bankruptcy auction to acquire the assets of The Sharper Image and paid $49 million-plus.

In August 2009, Camelot Venture Group secured the rights to operate a new Sharper Image catalog and website, *sharperimage.com*, and appointed David Katzman as CEO.

Two years later, while they continued to operate the catalog and website, Iconix Brand Group bought The Sharper Image brand and control of all licensing agreements.

In June 2014, Camelot Venture Group acquired the rights to the catalog and e-commerce from Iconix Brand Group. The brand rights still remained.

In December 2016, California-based ThreeSixty Group, owners of the FAO Schwarz brand, purchased The Sharper Image brand licensing rights from Iconix Brand Group for $100 million.

The Sharper Image name was used to sell products through third-party retailers, including Best Buy, Bed Bath & Beyond, Office Max, and Big 5 Sporting Goods. New products were created through partnerships with other businesses.

The bank creditors said the biggest asset of any of these transactions was the use of the brand name, The Sharper Image. The biggest allocation of money—$100 million—was put toward the name *The Sharper Image.*

So this is why I feel it's so important to take time to think about a clever and creative company name along with a domain name that represents it well as you begin your endeavor.

TODAY'S CONSUMER EXPERIENCE
WITH THE SHARPER IMAGE BRAND

Today, The Sharper Image features products and promotions through multiple digital and traditional marketing channels, including TV commercials, email, and social media outlets. The website continues to showcase innovative and unique products, carrying both The Sharper Image name and other well-known brands. It is not the same as The Sharper Image of the past. We were really inventing new products, and introducing things that the world had never seen before, and at a high-quality level. We were a leader in innovative technology, often bringing new technology to the home for the first time. Later, after the bankruptcy, it became a licensing brand name, meaning the name was put on a product with the intention that the product would be perceived to be of high quality because it carried The Sharper Image name. Sometimes that is true, and many times it is just average in quality but has a good brand name. At least the name is valuable and living on!

THE BOTTOM LINE

The Sharper Image's bankruptcy was not driven by the economy but lack of product innovation. Levin's team did not understand merchandising well enough to come up with creative ideas. Private-equity people have often thought that retailing is an easy way to make money, and that smart ones can do it better than anyone.

What hubris! Retailing is a complicated business that takes experience. The most recent example of the misconception that anyone can play is Eddy Lampert, a billionaire financier who thought he could build Sears and Roebuck into a better business when he took over in 2013. Instead, it failed, and Sears declared bankruptcy five years later.

My entire experience since 2006 is still bittersweet. If the new owners had made the stock go to $100, I would have acknowledged that they were much smarter than me. As the founder of The Sharper Image, I found it disheartening to watch what happened to it. Of course, it was also difficult to see so many of the employees I both hired and befriended lose their jobs and their connection to the brand. I was also disappointed that the stores were gone. I had hoped my children would one day walk past a Sharper Image store and say, "Hey, my dad created that."

As it turned out, though, I have had one of the best periods of my life in the 14 years since being fired and leaving The Sharper Image. I have been fortunate to have the opportunity to pursue my hobbies. I have especially enjoyed pursuing my lifelong interest in investing in the stock market. My experience in evaluating retail concepts and products has given me a keen insight into what will succeed and grow, and what won't. As a result, I'm able to "see" which company's stock price will go up. This insight gives me an edge in investing, and that has translated into superior portfolio performance, which has been very exciting.

If you're interested in the stock market, you might be interested in my online investing community or my book, *Sharper Investing: Ditch Your Broker & Double Your Returns*. You'll find investing wisdom, stock picks, and specific trading examples designed to inspire the first-time investor as well as the seasoned investor. My goal is to empower you to skillfully trade options while reducing your risk and maximizing long-term gain. It's a unique and simple approach to portfolio management that you can master without a broker.

EXPERIENCE THE NOSTALGIA

Thank you for your connection to The Sharper Image brand, whether it was an experiential moment in one of our stores, fond memories from the catalog, or the pleasure of receiving a Sharper Image item. Thank you. I'm also grateful and delighted that you've taken an interest in learning more about The Sharper Image. I encourage you to go online to find so much of our rich history. Visit our extensive archive of nostalgic videos, featuring behind-the-scenes catalog-cover shoots with celebrity models, closed-door quarterly business meetings, and product library updates that were originally sent to the employees at The Sharper Image stores.

You can visit *RichardThalheimer.com* and my YouTube channel, where you'll find press releases and interviews and stories from former employees. In addition, on *TheLegendofSharperImage.com,* you'll have an opportunity to share your own story.

Here are those links and others:

TheLegendofSharperImage.com

RichardThalheimer.com

TheSharperFund.com—Private Family Fund

SharperInvesting.com—Options Trading & Investing

RichardSolo.com—Online Store

Social Media—*https://twitter.com/richard_solo*

SHARPER INVESTING: DITCH YOUR BROKER AND DOUBLE YOUR RETURNS

In preparation for my next book, I've taken what I've learned through decades of investing and made it accessible to investors via the web. I'll be sharing investing wisdom, stock picks, and specific trading examples that inspire the first-time investor as well as the seasoned investor as we grow *SharperInvesting.com*.

STORIES OF INNOVATION

TRACY WAN
President and Chief Operating Officer,
The Sharper Image, 1988–2006

*"Being in the center of the executive team as
former President and COO, I had an intimate
view of how moments of triumph and challenge
were successfully navigated with Richard and
the great teams at The Sharper Image."*

What a thrill it is to have this book, the website, and the
YouTube Channel available to relive the nostalgia of my
18 years at The Sharper Image. Those years were the best
years of my career. I can honestly say I am the luckiest
person to have had such wonderful opportunities when I
joined the company. I have always felt the highest sense

of pride when people ask me where I used to work. The responses from people are always phrases like, "I love The Sharper Image" or they launch into a story of their hands-on experience in one of the stores. This always happened during my tenure and it was so extraordinary to sense the customers' relationship to this extraordinary brand.

My awe of The Sharper Image goes back to 1988, a little over a year after the company had its Initial Public Offering listed on the NASDAQ to become a public company. I can still vividly remember my interview with then CFO Bob Schultz for the position of manager of SEC financial reporting.

With the memorable, confirming handshake, Bob became my mentor and taught me so much about the retail business. In return, I vowed to do an excellent job for him, for Richard, and for the company with the SEC financial reporting. Prior to joining The Sharper Image, I worked in public accounting, became a CPA, and worked in the real estate investment syndication business.

The ensuing years were the most invigorating, fun, and fulfilling working years of my career. I'll quickly recap the roles so I can get to the fun part of sharing my fondest, most impactful experiences working alongside Richard and my colleagues. And Richard is always to us Richard or RT; not Rick, not Rich.

For 10 years, beginning in 1988, I rose through the financial ranks, advancing from Manager of SEC Financial Reporting to Assistant Controller, Controller, and then to the huge honor of Chief Financial Officer. In 1999, Richard tapped me to be the President and Chief Operating Officer—what a special role to take on! I felt nervous about the *big job*, yet I also felt confident that I had learned our business very well, coming through the financial ranks while working with Richard and other senior executives of The Sharper Image. I had worked with customer service, supply chain, eCommerce, and the quantitative side of merchandising, marketing, creative, and advertising. (Remember you can see a lot of special behind-the-scenes videos in the video section on this site and on YouTube. I loved those videos featuring Richard and Steve Jobs; they are so fun to watch!)

The most impactful skill that Richard has taught me is the ability to *always* act with the most current information, in both our professional and personal lives. He is masterful at this. Others may interpret Richard's skill and approach as a person who is always changing his mind. And, of course, he will be changing his mind to stay on course. He would regularly receive new information, which was vital for his presentiment, strategic decision-making and especially his artful navigation of choppy waters. Richard always has more current information than most because of who he is. He is always observing, learning, listening, and asking questions. He is the most inquisitive person that I have known. I have the impression that his mind is never turned off, even when he's sleeping.

Great Care with His Team and Family Values

Richard showed great sensitivity to each one of our management teams. He took the time to get to know us individually and put a lot of emphasis and energy into learning what we valued. Family has always been important to Richard, as it is for me.

Richard knew that I didn't care about golf, mountain biking, or other hobbies. He knew my family is the most important thing to me, so he always tried to shape my work life in harmony with my family life.

I observed he did this with everyone on our management team. Richard devoted some very valuable time by being an assistant coach on his daughter's middle school softball team when she was the pitcher. He always managed to be there. His work/life balance always included his family.

Richard, Hard to Get Along with?

There were many times that I was asked, "How can you work with Richard for that long? Isn't he a difficult boss?" The answer is Richard was great to work with, and yes, he can be a difficult boss at times (I think that's the case with most bosses; it is true for myself as well) if you are not measuring up to his expectations and working at the speed with which Richard processes.

Our working relationship was invigorating and rewarding. Richard is meticulous with each decision, his attention to detail is unsurpassed, and his ability to spot trends, and his creativity all worked together in his creation and expansion of the Great Americana Brand— The Sharper Image. I experienced over and over the way Richard would develop his trust in his employees, and then the working relationship would blossom. But the employee would have to earn his trust through their own diligent conduct and ability to produce results. This is one of the ways he was able to recruit and maintain his loyal and independent, intelligent employees.

Sharper Image Design—Invented Here!

I will always remember the first time I joined our Sharper Image Design team at the remote offices in Marin County, California—the "secret skunkworks" location where the Sharper Image Design team got their creative juices flowing during dynamic sessions with Richard. Burritos were served on paper plates for lunch.

The Sharper Image Design team would spitball ideas for the next generation of our Sharper Image Design proprietary products. Some of these products included the Turbo Groomer, the famous nose hair trimmer, the Sound Soother with an astonishing 30 sounds (the most sounds was 12 before this), and the Ionic Hair Wand (an ionic hairbrush that brings out the shine in your hair). The design team also created the Shower Companion CD Player, a water-resistant CD player that you could hang in your shower! This was revolutionary back in the day, and there was nothing else like it. Nothing was too crazy to brainstorm. Richard knew that anything could be made. But the conversation always came back to reality—what would be the retail price? Can we get 75 points of margin at that retail?

Richard assembled the best group of talent for Sharper Image Design. The team was headed by Chuck Taylor, who is literally a rocket scientist from Honeywell; second in command was Andrew Parker, a Stanford-educated engineer. We had our own manufacturing experts led by Tom Krysiak, industrial designers, electrical and mechanical engineers, and graphic designers.

We coined the slogan "Invented Here" for Sharper Image Design products because they were truly invented in Marin County, California, just a quick trip across the Golden Gate Bridge from the corporate office. How cool is that?

Product details such as the color of the LED on the product (blue, or white, or green), the color of the finishing, and what type of battery the unit would run on were all important elements for great product design. These key details were all hashed out over burritos by Richard and the team. Sharper Image Design proprietary products gave us the competitive advantage of exclusive products, reinforced our brand as the leader in cool products, and provided us with the financial benefit of bigger margins.

Bold and Bright Creative for Memorable Product Packaging

Bold, bright, attractive creative was quintessential and synonymous with The Sharper Image products, catalogs, and website. Richard loved this part of the business and pretty much retained all creative control while leveraging on a very talented team of creative directors, photographers, graphic artists, copywriters, and production talents. This creative process also provided for gorgeous product packaging for our Sharper Image Design products, which made for great displays in our stores.

Thrive in the Face of Adversity

Like many retail businesses, there were ups and downs in our business. I recall when it was early in my tenure at Sharper Image, and we had a very tough year during one of the recession years. Our first nine months of operations that year had larger losses than we had expected. We needed to come up with a plan to regain sales and profits.

Richard went to trade shows as often as he saw the need to. He would find unusual products and always bring back good stories. One story he waited to tell us until *after* the results came. Well, during this down-turned year, Richard went to a tradeshow, doing what he favors to do at trade shows—he made a straight-line dash to the hall where the smaller display booths are. These are not well-known product companies, and they pay less to be in the smaller booths in the less-trafficked halls of the trade show.

Richard could always see the potential of the products from some of these lesser-known companies, and he proved it over and over again. (The original Razor Scooter, sold exclusively by Sharper Image in the beginning, was one of them!) At this trade show, he met a small manufacturer that made his product in his own small factory in Pittsburg, PA. This manufacturer had a gel insole product that provided cushioning inside shoes. Richard asked the owner about the product specs and the cost per pair if Richard were to order some large quantities.

Shortly after, in a company presentation to all of us, and earlier to our Board of Directors, Richard said persuasively, "It's the fourth quarter, and we have to score!" He pulled the gel insole out of his jacket pocket and let us know this was the answer. There was a moment of silence.

Then, Richard looked around at the team—he knew we didn't understand, and we probably looked a little skeptical. Richard said, "This gel insole will be a great seller. It's made right here in the USA. We can get adequate stock quickly. It's at the right retail price and a great margin. Only $19.95 with a 75 percent margin!

He and Craig, our president at that time, had done a casual survey with visitors in The Sharper Image stores to gauge interest, at the $19.95 price point. The Sharper Image Gel Insole was popular in the casual survey. Well, it turned out, Richard was and is a marketing prodigy—he was right!

He created the tagline "Let Your Feet Take a Vacation" and put three inexpensive chairs in each store so customers could sit down and sample the Gel Insole in their shoes. Then he compensated our salespeople for each pair they sold and, voila—we *sold* hundreds of thousands of pairs and made significant margin dollars to shore up the next year. Whew. That was a close one.

What Sells A Product:
Sales Headlines and Story Telling!

Richard taught me to appreciate the art and skill of storytelling and sales headlines. To entice a consumer, Richard always uses the approach of emphasizing the benefits and features.

Copy included the answers to questions such as: What does the product offer? How does that matter to the customer? The skills of sales headlines, written product copy, and immersive storytelling were a big part of Richard's consumer product marketing.

I recall one of our Sharper Image Design/Invented Here products, the Power Tower. The sales headlines were so vivid in describing what the product did, and why the customer would want it.

The product copy featured Richard saying, "How many CDs do you have that are scattered on your bookshelf that you wish were well organized? Here is the Power Tower— you easily put your CDs into each slot of the rotary tower, and with a press of a button, the CDs are brought up to your view, without you having to get down on your hands and knees to retrieve the CDs on the bottom of the rotary."

Now, that's good copy. There are hundreds of cool, powerful sales headlines, and copy for our products that were presented in the catalog, online, and in our stores. And that was just one of our reasons for success.

Need for Speed

So—it's true, Richard loves airplanes (yes, he's a pilot), motorcycles, and various fast cars. Yet, there's the safety-first side of Richard at the same time. Richard loved his Toyota Sienna minivan, too.

MENSA—One Last Personal Revelation

When I was a young controller, I was invited to most of the senior management team meetings and board meetings. I always prided myself on having a good memory and being meticulous with the financial operations.

One time at a meeting with Richard and the then CFO, Richard pointed to a figure and said that it didn't look quite right. I stared at it for a quick moment and said that I was pretty sure that it was correct. Richard smiled and just said quietly to me to double-check that later and let him know. Of course, right after the meeting, I immediately went back to my office and checked on the figure. Sure enough, I was wrong; Richard was right.

He is so sharp with figures, and his financial acumen is extraordinary. Of course, Richard could easily run the finances of the company, but that would not be putting his talents to best use. As I reflect on my working relationship with Richard, I believe the yin and yang that made it work so well for 18 years was that Richard enjoyed and excelled at the creative process and unrelentless belief in his vision, while I enjoyed and excelled in the execution and quantitative aspects of our business, while believing in his unrelentless vision. It's a pleasure to work alongside such greatness.

Staying Connected, Years Later

I look forward to the quarterly dinners I still have with Richard and our former CFO Jeff Forgan, who is known for being quite funny. The three of us shared a lot of times together, both good and equally as tough, in the decade that we operated the company.

Richard has maintained the connection with us and continues to participate in these dinners, even a decade after we have moved on. It's always a good time to be with him—we put up our favorite stock picks, gossip about the celebrities, speculate on real estate, update on our children, and grimace about the political landscape as we drink good wines that Richard brings. Then we Uber home. I hope this goes on and on and on.

Current Days

I founded and operate the TYW Consultants LLC, a boutique advisory and consulting firm. We provide executive and board strategic advisory services, as well as consulting services for operations, financial, and the full business spectrum that makes a business thrive. I attribute a huge part of the success of my current professional life to the years of experience I accumulated from being on The Sharper Image executive team.

TONY FARRELL

Former Senior Vice President of Creative Services,
The Sharper Image, 1998–2008

Tony talks about the business insights and life
lessons he came away with from working with
Richard Thalheimer, "America's Gadget Guy."

Tony Farrell had a ringside seat to Richard Thalheimer's creative vision in action. He believed that Richard was not building a business but a community.

"He really wanted to share his enthusiasm with other people, and that comes through. He wasn't doing it just to sell it."

Part of that connection with his customers was Richard's ability to have faith in a product, be agile, and think outside the box. As Tony puts it, "A great merchant is one who does a lot of stuff on instinct and also moves quickly."

One of Richard's most enduring legacies was making it cool for men to shop by catalog. Tony believes he achieved that by including so much of himself on the catalog pages. "It was all Richard's taste, his personal taste." That taste extended to the catalog copy, which was very distinctive and originally crafted wholly by Richard himself. In that descriptive copy, Richard's genuine curiosity about and love for the products shone through. As Tony recalls an early Sharper Image catalog, "It was like a whole long classic, 2,000 words of direct marketing copy, this wonderful copy. All genuine, all super enthusiastic."

Moreover, in keeping with a marketing visionary, Richard's taste and style was not static but able to shift with the times. Tony notes how in the '80s, The Sharper Image catalog was full of extravagance and glitz, but by the '90s it had become more practical and simplified in feel and voice.

Like all members of The Sharper Image team alumni, Tony was captivated by Richard's aura and the heady and enjoyable business culture it created. "He was having fun, and he wanted you to have fun." Tony particularly remembers extravagant store manager dinners. These were like Oscars award ceremonies with everyone dressed to the nines and complete with big screens, loud music, and elaborate Razor Scooter table centerpieces.

"Richard's sense of style, his sense of entertainment, but more of it was about showing respect to these people, these store managers." Tony saw that Richard cleverly used occasions like this to both say thank you to individuals and motivate the team to work above and beyond—and it worked! "People will do anything for him. He really understood that just paying attention to people and recognizing them."

Richard's ability to energize people for the brand was not saved for one day a year; it was part of daily working life at The Sharper Image. The laser-like focus Richard gave to his team's personal and professional needs was exceptional. "Richard just always knew who people were, no matter where they were on the team, and he recognized them. He was always absolutely alert to where people fit in, where they were good, where they were weak."

These unusual management skills extended to an unparalleled level of empathy for his employees' work/ life balance that Tony experienced directly. "Half of 2006, I worked from home because we couldn't leave my daughter alone. He was just incredibly sympathetic and supportive and helpful."

Above all, Tony was left with an incredible sense of pride and gratitude to have been part of The Sharper Image story. Richard's passionate belief in the ability of his products to do good, make people more productive, and live better and healthier lives rubbed off big-time on his colleagues and customers.

That integrity was demonstrated by Richard's determination to stand behind his products with full refunds and to actively solicit customer feedback. Tony reminds us that most Sharper Image catalogs included this remarkable pledge. *If you'd like to share your thoughts directly with me about our stores, catalogs, web site, or products, I welcome your email....* He finished that sentence with his personal email address underscoring the value he placed on personal service and connection.

JOE WILLIAMS
Executive Vice President and former Chief Security Officer, The Sharper Image, 1985–2006

Joe describes why "quirky" delivered success at The Sharper Image and how his long working relationship with Richard became a valued personal friendship.

Richard: "If you get this job, what will you do for my company?" Joe: "I'm probably going to put a lot of your employees in jail." Richard: "I like that."

From that startling honesty, I developed a trust that has endured for over 30 years and immeasurably enriched the lives of both men.

As Joe tells it, "He started to look at me as someone he could really trust. That created a bond that we kept forever."

Joe and Richard worked together hand-in-glove for 22 years, and Joe's pride in their partnership is obvious. "I was featured in CSO magazine on the importance of a successful CSO working closely with the CEO. The picture that's used in the article is of he and I sitting in the hangar where the airplanes were."

Those airplanes (and motorcycles and cars, too) were a key element of the bond that developed between the two innovators as they worked and traveled together over the years. It was a bond where the lines between boss and employee took a back seat to mutual respect and friendship. Joe recalls, "I was going to buy an airplane. Richard came to me, and instead of me buying one, I started partnering with him." In that partnership, they flew together all over the US and Joe managed the maintenance of the planes. Those flights were special times when Richard and Joe were able to connect as admirers of airplanes and American landscapes while escaping the daily stresses of their roles.

Joe attributes much of Richard's success in business to his innate curiosity about things and ideas. He remembers a conversation when Richard explained, "When you love the product, you become interested in who thought of that product, who designed that product, where did that idea come from?" That unending curiosity was part of Richard's distinctive persona, which he owned with pride in his "QUIRKY" license plate. Joe believes that Richard's unique way of looking at the world set The Sharper Image apart from competitors. "No one could do the things that he did as well as he did. Nobody. A lot of people tried, and a lot of people failed."

Joe respected that while Richard was clearly a creative visionary, he also understood the importance of attention to detail, which was critical to Joe's own role in security. "He's very precise in everything he does and it shows in flying."

While Richard clearly had a talent for playing *"big"* when it came to products and stores and was happy to boost the brand with appearances on TV, Joe noted that he was remarkably humble in person. "He will brag about the success of the company. But personally, he doesn't like to draw attention. He didn't want to drive around in a stretch limo in New York; he didn't want people looking at him."

A career in security will tend to make people focus on the "glass-half-empty," and Joe was no exception—until he met Richard. "Richard always tends to see the good in everybody. He taught me that a lot of times, people are trustworthy and they're not all crooks."

That optimistic "glass-half-full" spirit most impressed Joe immediately after Richard's tenure as CEO of The Sharper Image ended abruptly. Joe was outraged on Richard's behalf, but that was not the way Richard chose to handle the difficult situation. As Joe recalls, "Rather than go somewhere and dwell on it and be upset and mad and angry, he just leaned into it. He just accepted what was and made the best of it."

Joe attributes Richard's tremendous resilience—the same resilience that allowed Richard to build The Sharper Image and steer it successfully for so many years—to Richard's pragmatic understanding that business has its inevitable ups and downs. Taking those cycles personally will not serve you or the business.

Joe Williams most admires Richard's ability to keep what really matters in perspective. He can still hear Richard's voice saying, "We're in good shape, and I've got a good family. I love where I live. Let's go ride motorcycles and fly airplanes."

JOSH TRETAKOFF
Former Senior Manager, Digital Media, The Sharper Image, 1998–2008

In a 10-year span, this store clerk rises through the ranks, being molded by Richard and the team, and later being the inception point as the first Digital Media Manager, launching the original Sharper Image website.

Josh moved up the ranks at The Sharper Image, beginning as a stock clerk in 1998, then cashier to senior sales and later promoted to store manager, Ghirardelli Square, San Francisco, and Marketplace Center, Boston. His last position was the first Digital Media Manager, ending in 2008.

From Josh:

It was my 10th birthday. I saw a full-page ad in a magazine by my dad's chair, showing a watch as I'd never seen. The ad went on and on about how many things the watch could do, and I was hooked. Every month after that, I looked for The Sharper Image ads, and the picture of the man who was bringing these marvelous things to life, Richard Thalheimer, and I told my parents that someday, I wanted to be just like him. Little did I know how influential he would be in my life.

Fast forward. It's the summer of 1998, and the new Sharper Image store in Boston has lines of eager customers, like me, outside. A security guard keeps the folks lined up so that the store is not overcrowded. I'm in line, waiting for my turn to actually see and touch the baubles from the future that The Sharper Image has only shown me in glossy catalogs before now.

The stanchions and ropes keep us practically pressed to the glass. It's my turn, and I'm moving around in this interactive museum of gadgets, gizmos, and toys, marveling at the fact that none are isolated out of my touch. As I look around, I hear the staff talking about their need for some help in the stockroom. I ask for an application, and my life is changed.

From that day forward, I was a man molded by The Sharper Image. I spent years in the stores, moving from a stock boy, all the way up to a store manager. I remember how proud I was when Richard himself visited, smiled at me, and presented me with my first gold award for exceptional sales performance. I wore that pin on my lapel for years, proudly.

During that time, I channeled my love of all gadgets beyond the store, immersing myself in the online world when I wasn't working. Back then, I spent hours with online communities, accessing through modems and phone lines, which led to managing one of the world's largest online communities. I could see the potential of this new network called the World Wide Web.

I wrote a proposal for Richard and Craig Womack to open a store in San Francisco; I was so enthused by the idea, I didn't even think of the insanity of having a store manager write a proposal for the CEO and president of a public company.

But during the next annual manager's meeting in San Francisco, Craig offered to meet with me for breakfast on two of the mornings to discuss. After we did, he said, "Josh, we definitely should do it. In about a year or two, we will."

Knowing that, I moved to San Francisco, so I would be there when Sharper Image was ready. Six months later, it was Christmas time. I was the store manager in Ghirardelli Square in San Francisco. It was early morning, and I was getting the store ready to open for the busy holiday, but it was quiet for the moment. I heard a tap on the glass front doors, and looked up: Richard Thalheimer, my inspiration, was standing there. Dumbfounded, I let him in.

He looked around, made some small talk, and then mentioned my proposal. He asked if I was ready to do what I proposed. My heart pounded. I looked him in the eye, and said, "Yes, I am." He smiled that smile that should be trademarked and told me that I should come to the corporate office next week.

The next six months were a blur. I started at the office, working for the incomparable Sydney Klevatt, who wanted nothing to do with this insolent 20-something who talked about the Internet, but he taught and learned, all at the same time. Richard came by one morning and asked us to go with him to a presentation at Yerba Buena from Steve Jobs, formerly of Apple.

We walked over, where Steve held court on the new software he was marketing, WebObjects, from his NeXT Computer Co. When Steve demonstrated that he could book a flight online, then pick up the phone and have it confirmed by the call center in real-time, he was sold. He turned to Syd and me and said: "Let's see if we can use that."

Funny aside: Years later, I learned that the demo on stage was typical of Jobsian smoke and mirrors. That call center Steve called on stage? It was actually to his assistant backstage on a cell phone. Steve never let facts be the obstacle to a great vision.

As our Internet business boomed, Richard came by my desk one day and led me to my new office. He was so pleased to see how floored I was and excitedly said, "Let's go pick out some art for you." We dashed around the building for 15 minutes, as he looked in every office and every conference room until something caught his eye. He grabbed it off the wall (I honestly can't remember from where), and we walked it back to my office, where he proudly hung it for me. It was one of the most rite-of-passage moments I'd ever experienced and stands out today.

Richard was not by any means the easiest CEO; he demanded results, and he was quick to express his displeasure when I came up short. He was equally hyper-aware of how important it was to motivate his people.

I remember a day I let him down, and he (rightfully so) let me have it. The next morning, he came by my office and said, "I just want to let you know that you are one of the smartest people I think I've ever worked with," and left. I sat there, stunned, and redoubled my resolve to live up to that compliment.

The hardest decision I ever made came a couple of years later, when I had the opportunity to join a startup in the dot-com boom. I labored over that decision for weeks. I didn't want to leave TSI, but it was too good of a chance. I remember when Richard learned I was leaving, and he greeted me with a wan smile, a shake of his head, and that "Josh...really?" that only he could pull off with both sincere honesty and friendly mocking. He wished me well, and I couldn't help but feel like I was leaving home for the first time.

Over the next few years, I found every way possible to work with The Sharper Image, doing partnerships and deals. I was back in the office for one such meeting, and Richard walked by the conference room I was in. He stopped short, flung the door open and said, "Josh, are you coming back?" with that enthusiasm that only Richard could muster. I wistfully replied that I was not, and he said: "Oh, well...worth a try!" And off he went.

JENNY WILLIAMS
Marketing, The Sharper Image,
2000–2008

An internal view of the extraordinarily visually appealing place to work from a member of Sharper Image's marketing team.

The Sharper Image corporate office was an exciting, inspiring place to work. It felt like a planned community designed to spark creativity and excellence—making it a place you wanted to be and contribute your best work.

The backdrop was sleek, color-coordinated furnishings, uncommon in most offices, particularly in the retail industry where the office is considered "back of the house." Throughout the space, Richard shared his collectibles, artwork, and colorful, eclectic gadgets.

Visually memorable are the lighted jukebox, neon sculptures, child's airplane barber chair, specialty Harley-Davidson motorcycles, life-size Star Wars characters, autograph of Abraham Lincoln and, of course, the suit of armor.

No vendor or visitor failed to comment that it must be a great place to work—and they were right.

FEDERICO DE BELLEGARDE

Former Senior Vice President of Licensing,
The Sharper Image, 1989–1993/1995–2015

With a 26-year tenure, this executive connected the team culture of The Sharper Image to a great sports team striving to sync up at the right time and sustain the performance.

My 26-year Sharper Image journey started in Boston on Patriots' Day 1989 and ended in April 2015 in NYC. However, it has never truly ended due to the experiences, camaraderie, great memories, and genuine affection for the many talented lifelong friends I worked with over the years and beyond.

Richard created and fostered an enduring legacy, and The Sharper Image, in its first incarnation, was much more than a direct marketing product or retail story. The culture of constantly striving for perfection down to the most minute detail across a host of disciplines was akin to a great sports team syncing at the right time and sustaining the performance. We mostly synced perfectly, while at other times not so much, but the sense of being in this together cultivated a genuine pride of being associated with such a fun, well-managed organization. We worked hard, played hard, respected each other, laughed, struggled, and always enjoyed the reaction when you told someone you worked at The Sharper Image. *"I love that store!"* was a typical response, and we soaked it up!

In August 2018, Richard hosted a Sharper Image 10-year post-bankruptcy reunion, and 100-plus former co-workers came from all over the world to once again share each other's company and regale the many stories of The Sharper Image past.

Today, while the brand lives on, the "Richard Thalheimer years," and the many folks that collaborated in the journey made for a wonderful and meaningful chapter in so many of our lives.

ANDREW PARKER

Director, Product Development, The Sharper Image;
Senior Vice President, Sharper Image Design; Senior Vice
President, Engineering and Technology, 1999–2008

*"Richard was unmatched at identifying the risks
worth taking and he always brought fun and
challenging ideas to the internal design team. It
was a once-in-a-lifetime opportunity."*

I was very lucky to be part of the "skunkworks" Sharper
Image Design team in Novato. Every product designer
wants to work on exciting new things, and Richard
always brought us fun and challenging ideas. He was
unmatched at identifying the risks worth taking. Not
every idea made it into production, and not every new
product sold a million pieces. But, in baseball terms, we
got to swing at many pitches, we had lots of base hits,
and we enjoyed some amazing home runs! Our team of
creative, fun people inspired one another to do our best
work. Together, we generated a portfolio of hundreds of
innovative products, covered by hundreds of patents,
and drove huge growth in sales and margins.

Richard understood his customers and their delight in
discovering new items. He made sure that every new catalog cover compelled customers to look inside, visit the

website, or enter a store. Many of those cover products were extravagant, but they drew customers in, where they'd discover fun gifts and practical items that anyone could buy.

After Richard left, the new management team did not understand the company or what had made it successful. They were terrified of risk—and didn't have any ideas—so they stopped us from developing our own new items.

XAVIER ESTRADA
Art Director, The Sharper Image, 1999–2008

"For most, The Sharper Image was an exciting and inspiring place to work. For me, it was much more than that. It was the beginning of my career as a designer and a lifelong friendship with Richard!"

I was 21 years old when I started working at The Sharper Image. I was finishing my senior year in design school when I was hired by Joseph Tsang, the creative director at the time, who was later promoted to VP. He was one of the most extraordinary bosses and still a very close friend today.

There I was, working at my dream job, straight out of school. I couldn't believe it!

The Sharper Image stores were full of such cool stuff. We were like kids in a candy store! In the creative department, we were lucky to see the latest and greatest products before the public ever did. It was a life of "sneak peeks." In fact, I distinctly remember when the segway was first introduced to the world. Yep, we played with it first at the office.

The headquarters office, where I worked, was so visually over the top. It was like nothing I had ever seen, other than in the movies. It was truly an extraordinary and surreal place to experience and work in, even the simple walk through the building from department to department.

I met so many great people working there. I learned so much from all of these talented artists, for which I'm eternally grateful to this day. Each person seemed to be handpicked, and we shared a feeling of family-focused fun with a greater vision for everyone.

One of the great highlights for me was my first interaction with Richard, which grew into a relationship where we worked side by side. I remember being terrified of him, especially when he came into the creative department. I would try to be as invisible as I could. Until one day I was working through the lunch hour, and I was the only one in the department. I was working on a new concept ad for the Ionic Breeze. The concept was routed to Richard for review, and as usual, it was filtered back through Tony Farrel to me with all edits and comments so I could prepare the next draft.

Well, not that day! He came straight into the creative department, directly to my desk, where I was "plugged in" listening to music on my headphones and working on the ads. When I looked up, I thought, "Holy cow, he is looking right over me at the screen." I completely froze. Very politely, he asked if he could make some changes to the copy.

I was terrified. I told him that all ad copy needed to be approved by Tony. He gently and firmly replied, "Don't worry about it; I'm telling you to change it."

And then he chuckled with an intense look that communicated, "Please, do what I want now." I was so nervous. I made all the edits he requested. I printed it out for him as quickly as I could. He was impressed with the speed I was able to generate in order to complete it for him. He thanked me, and he left happily with his new edited version. After he left and I gathered my thoughts, I said to myself, "Oh, wow, my first Richard encounter, so exciting, and nerve-wracking; what the heck just happened? That was awesome!"

From that day on, I was on his radar, and he knew my name. He continued to drop by my desk and ask to make edits on the fly all the time after that day. And so it began, a closer relationship with Richard.

He has been an inspiration to me through the years. He was the driving force in pushing my limits to his higher standards, whether working on the catalogs, filming product videos, or creating unique packaging for Sharper Image Design and RichardSolo Products. We also share the same creative aspirations and tastes, which makes working with him a designer's dream.

Most of all, I am so proud of the great things we accomplished together at The Sharper Image. We created a body of work that was revolutionary at the time. We pushed the limits of the technology available to us then. We pioneered a lot of the design work seen today in major brand advertising.

My journey continued: I have had the pleasure to work with Richard, present day, in his venture RichardSolo as well as participate in the photo collection and design for this book. We have worked together and formed a lifelong friendship. Working with Richard has been an adventure and experience I treasure. It's like a family for me. It continues to be a pleasure to experience Richard's pull of excellence, coupled with his incredible genius.

TOM KRYSIAK

Senior Vice President, Sharper Image Design, 1996–2008

*Tom provides an inside account of working
within the "optimistic synergy" of the design
and innovation team at The Sharper Image.*

It's hard to believe that a nondescript office park in
Novato was the front of much of Richard Thalheimer's
brilliance blended with genuine and raucous fun. Those
twice-weekly sessions started many times with Richard
bringing in a dozen High-Tech Burritos. Product topics
were always free-form. There was fast-moving, simul-
taneous ideation via Tristan's quick sketches, while Ed
would quickly fabricate a simulation or concept model
with the help of our nearby model maker. After that, two
more team members would figure out electronic circuit
details and the theoretical QA specs in just a few days.
And at the same time, a group of us could wrestle over
product costs, features, patent applications, and which
Asian vendor would be best suited to build and ship the
new creation properly.

Indispensable Mark always came up with the best tag
lines and would contribute the greatest "out of the box"
product embellishments. Lastly, the hugely important
technical legacy issues, applied material sciences, and

legal precedents were presided over by the EVP who was fond of selecting and stabbing vendor donated chocolates (always for emphasis) with a mini-screwdriver!

Those fun meetings concluded with many detailed pages of to-do, careful technical inquiries, and vendor follow-ups for scores of those high margin, unique Sharper Image Design products. We all enjoyed Richard's incomparable creativity, our team's optimistic synergy, and the rewarding excitement of bringing life to a new RT inspired creation.

Yes—we could build anything! And undoubtedly, these were our finest years.

JOE CHEN

Quality Manager, The Sharper Image, 2002–2008

Joe found that working in the field of his interest translated to working on things he felt excited about— and working with a team that he considered friends.

Before I joined The Sharper Image, I was in the midst of a personal low point in life. In the span of two weeks, I had the pleasure of buying a larger car in anticipation of the birth of my son and just 14 days later getting laid-off from my job.

On top of that, a few years before, we had just bought a new home, and the mortgage payment was hefty. With these new circumstances, the helplessness I felt was at times overwhelming.

In the summer of 2002, I joined The Sharper Image as the manager of quality and a member of The Sharper Image Design team. This was my first foray into consumer products.

With help and guidance from Tom Krysiak and Andrew Parker, my transition into The Sharper Image family was smooth and joyous. As time went on, I only enjoyed my work more and more. I've always listened to advice saying it's essential to work in the field of one's interest. It's what I would call it when you are also working on things you feel excited about! The Sharper Image Design products we developed were cutting edge and ahead of the curve. Most importantly, the most interesting thing as well as the best thing I learned from Richard was that every product had and needed to have a great story! That's what made people love the products.

The Sharper Image Design team was filled with great people; it felt like I was working with great friends! I truly enjoyed every day going to work at The Sharper Image.

I have also turned on all of the air purifier samples from Sharper Image that I kept for sentimental reasons. Of course, I am not suggesting that the air purifiers are the solution to COVID-19, but I feel much better having them working!

JOHNNY YOTNAKPARIAN
District Manager, The Sharper Image
Senior Vice President of Sales, The Sharper Image,
1998–2008

"The limo ride of a lifetime started with the back window slowly rolling down, and a mystical, yet real, man of genius welcoming me to an extraordinary 10-year career."

One of my fondest memories of Richard is one of my first memories. After first interviewing with Craig Trabeaux, an appointment was made for me to meet with Richard Thalheimer! The man, the myth, the legend! I was so nervous.

Craig gave me an address of where to meet Richard on Fifth Avenue in NYC. There I am, nervous as heck (did I fail to mention a hurricane was about to hit within six hours?!). A long black Limo pulls up, the window slowly comes down, and Richard pops his head out, with his trademark smile and says, "You must be Johnny Y, hop in!"

Is this a kidnapping or an interview? Talk about a captive audience! Richard was so nice and cordial. He was really interested in my background, yet he also made me feel relaxed and comfortable, like the interview was only a formality. We talked about my experience, my family, and my goals. Storm clouds rolled in, and Richard was as calm as could be. We went to visit a new potential location, talking the whole time. Before you know it, two hours had flown by, and we pulled up in front of the newly renovated 57th Street store.

"I have a plane to catch before the storm comes in. So nice to meet you. I am sure we will meet again," he said with a wink and a smile.

Craig called me back before I made it home and said, "Welcome aboard!"

I am so appreciative of Richard for welcoming me to his Sharper Image family, where I met so many special people whom I still keep in touch with today! Thank you, Richard—all the best!

The Sharper Image 1979 Catalog

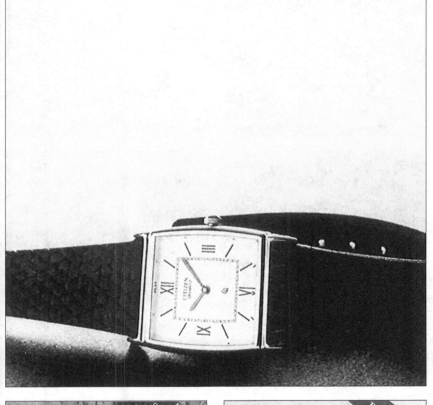

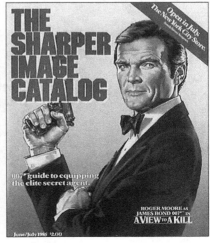

Take home an American beauty.

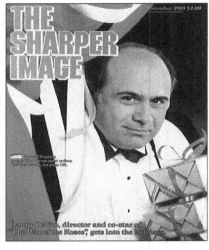

December 1989 $2.00

Danny DeVito, director and co-star of
"The War of the Roses", gets into the holidays.

Summer 1992

Welcome home
the boys of
summer (p. 6).

See John Goodman in
"The Babe" from
Universal Pictures.

Over 150 products under $100!
Order direct.
1-800-344-4444

■TRAVEL
■MASSAGE
■OUTDOOR FURNITURE
■POOL INFLATABLES
■HEALTH AND FITNESS

Fitness comes home.
With a new generation of
advanced equipment
for body conditioning
without compromise.
See pages 19–29.

September 1985 $2.00

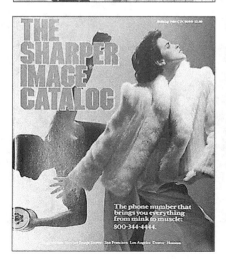

The phone number that
brings you everything
from mink to muscle:
800-344-4444.

June 1989 $1.00

Make Father's Day
come alive.

Order toll-free
800-344-4444

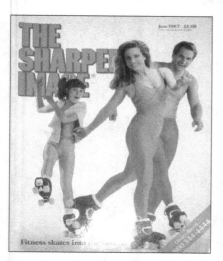

THE SHARPER IMAGE

June 1987 $1.00

Fitness skates into [...]

THE SHARPER IMAGE CATALOG

HOLIDAY 1985   CDC 00449 $2.50

Phone for giants, page 4.
Knife worth a ten year wait, page 9.
Newest notebook computer champion, page 11.
Color slides in five minutes, page 12.
A real pet robot, page 63.
A pricing policy second to none. See order form.

THE SHARPER IMAGE CATALOG

Christmas 1992 $2.00

Free 1-800-344-4444

THE SHARPER IMAGE CATALOG

Park your favorite dream car on your desk. See page 4.

Fall 1984 / DC 00449 $2.00

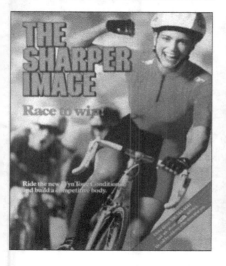

THE SHARPER IMAGE

Race to win.

Ride the new Lifecycle conditioner and build a competitive body.

THE SHARPER IMAGE CATALOG

Open April 25th
The Washington D.C. store.

May 1985 $2.00

Technology's new wave: peer into the future.

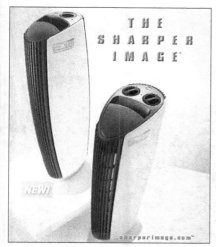

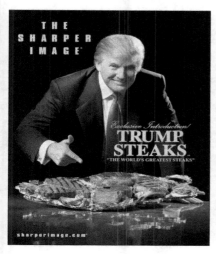

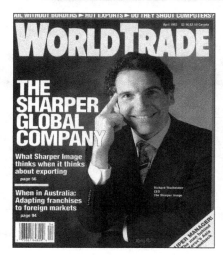

IT'S
in the
MAIL!

*Once limited to the United States,
mail-order companies are entering the global
marketplace — led by mid-sized firms like
The Sharper Image and Patagonia.*

By Art Garcia

Sharper Image's Richard Thalheimer: Take that

Fairchild's EXECUTIVE TECHNOLOGY

Business Strategies for Retail Industry Leaders

Limited Fortifies
Infrastructure to
Support Family
Brand Growth

Sharp Shooting

The Sharper Image takes aim at expanding
its customer base through interactive 'sticky'
Web technologies

San Francisco Chronicle

BUSINESS

"There was a point when it was hard to grow beyond the original 45 to 50
street in high-end areas. Now the product is a little more practical."

Shifting gears

Sharper Image pitching a line of more practical products
that are designed to appeal to mainstream shoppers

When The Sharper Image began selling products via mail
order in the late 1970s, its array of electronic gizmos was a
huge success. But as the decade of greed gave way to a
decade of moderation, this catalog and retail company
found itself losing ground. It rebounded by using an old-
fashioned recipe—listening to customers.

THE CUTTING EDGE

Retailing has a long history in Richard
Thalheimer's family. His great-grandfather,
a German immigrant, started a horse and
livery service in Little Rock, Ark., in the
1890s.

LOOKING SHARP:
Richard Thalheimer demonstrates
the Pulse Action Fans Massager,
a new product designed
by The Sharper Image.

By Nancy
Kennedy

Photographs
by Tom Graves

The Sharper Image

To better reflect its high-tech image and attract younger buyers, the cataloger/retailer sharpened its Website

By Leslie Goff

The Sharper Image's sharper image

By Gretchen Morgenson

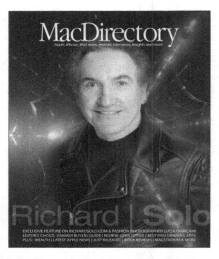

MacDirectory
Apple, iPhone, iPad, news, reviews, interviews, insights and more

Richard | Solo

EXCLUSIVE FEATURE ON RICHARDSOLO.COM & FASHION PHOTOGRAPHER LUCIA GIANCANI
EDITOR'S CHOICE: SUMMER BUYERS' GUIDE | REVIEW: OPEN OFFICE | BEST IPAD DRAWING APPS
PLUS: HEALTH | LATEST APPLE NEWS | JUST RELEASED | BOOK REVIEWS | MACSTADIUM & MORE

CPSIA information can be obtained
at www.ICGtesting.com
Printed in the USA
LVHW020828031220
673100LV00004B/67

9 781544 517902